Children
OF
Mercy

TALES AND TEACHINGS
FROM THE WORLD
— OF —
INDEPENDENT MUSIC

EDITOR
RON TREMBATH

MARQUETTE BOOKS
SPOKANE, WASHINGTON

First Printing, March 2011
Printed in the United States

ISBN for this Edition
978-0-9833476-1-3

Printed by
MARQUETTE CUSTOM BOOKS
A Division of MARQUETTE BOOKS LLC
Spokane, Washington
www.MarquetteBooks.com

This book is dedicated to Gordon-Hjalmar Nyberg and every single man, woman, and child who has continued to be the brightest rays of sunshine into everyone they know even as they suffer every day from Cystic Fibrosis. As long they continue to fight to survive long enough to find a cure, we will continue to fight as well.

Also to the folks who truly embody the spirit of this book. To those with writing within the pages, and to those who are not. To the lost yet focused souls who are continuously using music to express themselves in a positive manner. Thank you for being the greatest subject one could ever consider creating a book about.

This book is also dedicated to the memory of Michael "Eyedea" Larsen and Rudolph Eberstadt IV. Geniuses taken before his time.

Table of Contents

5

Acknowledgments

Thank you –

Brenna & Danny Van Stone, Lars Kronfalt, Ryan Feigh, Curtis Sutton, Jason Michael Allred, Jeanne Betak Cleemann, George L. Evanson, Johanna Helenius, Ruby Mughal (of Bruno's Pizza in Longview, WA), Jackie & Nick Wengerd, Sergio Montes, Eric Fielding, Shawn Fogel, Fredrik Westerlund, Christopher Eaves, Joseph Gessert, Steven Laird, and Shawna Hopp.

Without your extremely gracious support during the Children of Mercy Kickstarter fundraising campaign, this project would have never found a place in this world, and the pages you are holding would have never been able to become real. Thank you all for making this dream a reality.

And an extra special thank you to an "anonymous" individual who also donated to the Kickstarter fundraising campaign. One very generous and loving grandfather has asked that his donation, the largest during the campaign, be given the name of his three granddaughters – Ava, Sophia, and Lelaina. Thank you Grandpa!

Introduction to Children of Mercy

The pages you hold in your hands are not the work of any one single individual. Rather it is the product of several individualistic members from the underbelly of the world of independent music. Each contributor in this book has their own story to tell. And while scenarios may seem to reoccur, these are real tales from the real people who have shaped the world of independent music today. These are our heroes.

Some of the lucky contributors are full time musicians who live and breathe music day in and day out either through performing, promoting, or being paid to listen. But, some are not. These are people you know. They are the one's checking out your books at the library, the one with the green hair. They serve up your Chi Latte's at Starbucks. They wash your cars, or recommend music choices at your local Target. They are real everyday people. But as the day turns to night, these everyday people get the chance to be stars. Whether they are ripping it up on guitars they bought on layaway, or writing to their heart's content at a Starbucks on a laptop they bought with a high interest in store credit card. They have dreams. They have passions. They have a dire love for independent music. And they want to share it with you in this book.

The journey you are about to embark on takes place in several different regions of the world. From Portland, Oregon to Copenhagen, Denmark. From Lawrence, Kansas, to Indonesia, and back to Martha's Vineyard, Massachusetts, back over to the UK, and many more. In fact, many of the words you are about to read were written by folks who do not call English their first language, and in some cases not even their second or third. But, they all had one common goal when it came to getting this book out to the world - to open the eyes to the outside world on how tough and sometimes demeaning it is to be a solely independent musician, as well as highlight why it might just be the only true way to be a real artist in the musical world. All the while, doing some real good for a wonderful cause.

When I began setting up this project in late August of 2010, I knew it was going to be a charity based effort. The problem was deciding what charity we would support. Then on one drunken rainy night in a hotel room in Wichita Falls, Texas, I received an e-mail from Ola Nyberg telling me his gut-wrenching story of his son Gordon-Hjalmar and his struggles with Cystic Fibrosis. From that moment on it would be decidedly known that this was the struggle we were going to try our damndest to fight. And through the power of independent music, we know we can make a difference in the lives of little GH, and thousands of others across the globe.

All proceeds, sales, and royalties of this book will be donated to the Cystic Fibrosis Foundation in the United States, as well as the Cystic Fibrosis Trust in the United Kingdom.

Thank you for taking this journey with us. I hope you enjoy the ride.

Ron Trembath
Editor/Coordinator

Introduction to Cystic Fibrosis
By Colleen Nyberg

Even while my son was still growing inside me, I began to develop hopes and dreams for my child. I thought about the life we would be bringing into the world, and what characteristics and values we would place importance on (creativity, intelligence, kindness and respect for all, honesty, etc.). I had originally been hoping for a little girl but when the doctor told me we would be having a son, I realized it didn't matter; I just wanted a healthy baby. That was all that was important. Unfortunately, that was not to be. My son was born with a genetic disease called Cystic Fibrosis (CF).

A little background information: Cystic Fibrosis is a progressive disease that affects thousands of people worldwide and has no cure. It mainly affects the respiratory and digestive systems but can also lead to problems in other parts of the body. In order to have Cystic Fibrosis, one must have inherited 2 of the cystic fibrosis gene (one from each parent). This defective gene causes the body to create a thick, sticky mucus that fills up the lungs and causes life-threatening lung infections. It also blocks the pancreas so the natural enzymes cannot help the body break down and absorb food properly. Just 50 years ago, children with Cystic Fibrosis rarely lived through their elementary school years but advances in research and treatments have lengthened the life expectancy of people with CF. Today, the average life expectancy is 37 years old.

Our son, Gordon-Hjalmar, was diagnosed at 6 months of age after severe weight loss (failure to thrive) and numerous testing. The life we live today is very different from the one I had envisioned during my pregnancy. An average day for my 2 year old son consists of several medications that are taken 3 times each day, extra vitamins taken daily, fat supplements taken several times per day, as well as inhalation treatments and physiotherapy that is done twice daily to help strengthen his body and expel phlegm. While his lung function is currently pretty good, he is pancreatic insufficient which means that he must also takes replacement enzymes with all his meals and snacks and also eat a high fat diet. We have a whole team of people we work closely with (a nutritionist, a physiotherapist, counselors, nurses, and Drs) to keep my son as healthy and strong as possible but hospital visits are a part of life for a person with Cystic Fibrosis, and we have had a few. In fact, whenever we step onto the children´s ward of the hospital, we are greeted warmly by a staff that knows us well.

While our life is different than the one we had anticipated, in many ways our little boy is just like any other 2 year old. He is curious and active and eager to explore the world around him. He loves to run and jump and play make believe. He enjoys looking at and listening to storybooks. He loves listening to music, dancing to music, and most of all, making his own music.

I admit that some days are overwhelming and emotional and just plain hard to get through but then I look at my sweet baby boy and find the strength to do what must be done and help him fight for the chance to grow up, experience the adventures of life, and make his own dreams a reality. With love and strength and determination, we live each day with the hope that one day CF will stand for Cure Found.

The following book is a project of love from creative individuals from all over the world. They have generously donated their various talents in an effort to raise funds and awareness for this devastating disease. I send heartfelt thanks to each and every one of them.

Time In The Sun
By Andy Botterill

We all have our time,
our moment in the sun,
days when the grass is green
and we too are healthy and strong,
our whole lives ahead of us,
it feels we can do anything

We're invincible.
Every dream is possible.
No path is yet excluded
Fueled by our youthful hope,
the world is at our feet.

You Can't Have The Highs Without The Lows
By Christopher Taylor

You can't have the highs without the lows. It is a malevolently cold night. It feels like the air is ripping at my skin. We set off for a gig in Leicester in a car with no heating. The heating hasn't worked for some time. One day it will be fixed. One day. The place we are due to play at is clearly not the city's premier rock venue. As these places often are, it is above a pub on a deserted back street. As they often do, the ghosts of better days seem to haunt both the pub and the venue. The pub is a large corner building with huge windows and what initially looks like an inviting winter warming glow, an impression that evaporates as soon as I walk in. There is nobody in there apart from what appears to be a few underage drinkers. There is a slight air of menace. I think that it seems very strange for a pub in a city centre to be empty on a Saturday evening. But then I remind myself that we are here for the sound check, it is early, there is plenty of time for the place to fill up.

    The nature of many venues that low- to-medium level bands play at around the UK has led to them being collectively named the "toilet circuit". Although some of the venues are (or were – many have now gone) places that appear to have been bypassed by such technical innovations as the vacuum cleaner, and do actually smell like toilets, others are decent venues that just happen to be on the same circuit that is regularly played by bands who are at a certain level. This place is definitely not in the latter group. If it really was a toilet, it would be one where you've got diarrhea and there's no paper or lock on the door. It is disgusting. It has obviously not been cleaned since around 1983. The fire escape is blocked and has a chair stuck in the bars, to create just that little bit of extra delay in the event of an emergency evacuation. Remnants of an ancient PA are strewn across the stage. It speaks of hopelessness, desolation and abandonment. This is our kind of place.

The promoter greets us in quite a jovial manner, perhaps to compensate for the obvious unease that is written across our faces. He reminds me of a larger, shaven-headed version of Damon Albarn from Blur, and has the requisite Britpop-era "cheeky geezer" manner. He has an almost lunatic optimism about him, in an "oh dear, somebody seems to have nicked half the PA but let's soldier on" kind of way. We sound check, and against the odds, Damon (who doubles up as the engineer in an unsurprising piece of cost cutting) makes us sound much better than we would have predicted, given the circumstances. Afterwards, the other two acts haven't arrived, so we sit down for a chat about "Whether We Should Accept A Major Record Deal Or Not".

When most bands discuss this, it is purely an academic question mixed with wishful thinking, as the number of major label offers on the table is usually zero. But for once we aren't just talking fantasist nonsense, as some major labels have actually contacted us recently. So, we are sitting at a clearly soon-to-be-packed venue in Leicester. Over the last couple of weeks, our album has received a rave review and a score of 8/10 in NME Magazine, and our first John Peel session has been broadcasted. At some point soon, tough decisions are going to have to be made. Are we going to stick to our indie roots and remain credible but sell only a fraction of the records we would potentially be able to? Or will we take Parlophone or Sony's cash, ride out the inevitable cries of "sell out!" and hopefully "do a Radiohead", combining huge success with a strong independent ethic while remaining reasonably cool? I wonder out loud if signing to a major will be a betrayal of our indie ideals, whether we could do it and stick to our highly valued "roots" (whatever they are), how major labels can stifle creativity and development and then spit you out after no time at all if you're not an immediate smash hit, and so on. In saying all this, I am very careful not to rule out signing to a major. I am just flagging up some points for discussion and thought. Damon looks at us as if we are idiots.

First on the bill is a man called Ben, a fellow artist on our record label. He is a solo singer-songwriter, a term which fills me with dread because it usually indicates something very bad. However, his music is a kind of spooky psychedelic folk that is well crafted and beautifully played. After sound checking, we walk down the road and bump into him outside Burger King, which he is about to enter. This seems rather prosaic for him. You expect spooky psychedelic folksters to exist on more mysterious sustenance than that which is available in the fast food emporia of Britain's 21st century identikit high streets. But spooky psychedelic folksters have to eat, and the choice on the dark fringes of Leicester's city centre is limited.

In a spirit of camaraderie, and to show support for a colleague with whom we share a label, I congratulate him on the high quality of his music. Somewhere within this I mention the name Nick Drake, saying to Ben that his music sometimes reminds me of him. As far as I am concerned, this is one of the highest compliments you can pay any musician. Three albums of beautifully sad, haunting and plaintive music that have never been matched, and an early death before the creative rot sets in. What better comparison? Rather than giving embarrassed thanks, Ben looks slightly annoyed by this and tells me in no uncertain terms that he does not think he sounds like Nick Drake. Oh dear. I know that most musicians don't like being compared to other artists, and I know I get sick of all the comparisons to Mogwai, but come on, we're talking about *Nick Drake.* It's not as if I accused him of sounding like The Wurzels.

Camaraderie slightly reduced, Ben announces that he is going to get his burger. I skulk off to somewhere slightly more sophisticated and Italian ("Pizzaland"). We return to the venue just after the doors open. I am not expecting queues around the block, a sold out gig and fans trying to get in by any means possible. But the silence in the street is worrying, and the pub seems even emptier than it was earlier. Perhaps I should do some last minute promotion. Scream "post-rock fans of Leicester, where are you?" into the darkness? Shove copies of our NME review into the faces of passers-by? What are you supposed to do? Back in the venue, there is a rather grim sight. Ben is about to take to the stage. The audience consists of us, Damon, the headline band and one of their girlfriends, and Alan from our record label. Not one person has paid to get in. Ben plays a 45-minute set. Usually, I would quite happily listen to his music for this length of time and longer. Tonight though, I am freezing and slightly miserable and I know that I face playing a gig to nobody followed by a long journey in a cold car. I just want it over and done with.

We take to the stage. As usual when nobody is watching us, we play a great set. I feel sorry for the headline band, which have yet to play to an empty room and have had even longer to contemplate doing so and what it means. We should probably stay and watch them, but we make excuses about the length of the journey back, which appear to be accepted. As we are leaving, two men walk by the venue. "Do they still have bands on there?" one asks the other while looking up towards the first floor where we have just played.

We drive back to London in the same icebox of a car. There will be both better and worse times than this. *You can't have the highs without the lows.*

Christopher Taylor *is a guitarist, songwriter and singer. He was born in Middlesbrough, England and now lives in London. He plays in The Workhouse, The Platers and Sad Wolf. The Workhouse have released two critically acclaimed albums, The End of the Pier and Flyover.*

...Or How Not To Lose Your Shirt In DIY
By Edward Bignar

"Art is making something out of nothing and selling it."
- Frank Zappa

There is absolutely no reason in the world why you should want to start your own DIY label. The odds are just stacked against you from the very beginning to even survive your first release. So if you think that you're going to be the next Saddle Creek, Sub Pop, Alternative Tentacles or even one of these trendy Italian labels that I'm too clueless to be able to name check, stop, don't even try. Because, honestly, it's probably just not going to happen for you.

If making money is your goal, I can guarantee you right now you're barking up the wrong tree. My eBayed book, record and movie collections can attest to that. The sad truth is most labels I've observed and lived more hand to mouth than all the artists and writers I've known combined, and you don't even get the added bonus of the romanticism of the craft. The girls don't swoon over your latest lathe release. DIY label owners are the nerds of the industry. DIY isn't sexy. No Sex. No Drugs (that have been offered to me anyway). All that leaves us with is the Rock N Roll. By Rock N Roll, I mean the 15 year old Xanex addicted sociopath "noise artist" who now has your home address and is chucking darts at your picture in his mommy's basement solely because you decided that his contribution didn't fit your latest compilation.

Do you still want to start a DIY label?

Well I tried my best to convince you otherwise, but that's what DIY is about, the passion the fire, the overwhelming *need* to get music heard. We are the geeks walking down the hallways of your high school trying to decide if they're going to listen to the copy of Blood Visions they dubbed off onto a tape the night before, or if they're going to listen to Doolittle for the 5 billionth time this week. It's not about anything more than musical OCD. We all have it, get used to it, here's the only advice that I can give you after all the years of running (and not running) a DIY label.

A famous filmmaker once noted that the first thing that anybody should do before even writing the script is to look around you and see what you have available. Because if you have 5 bucks and a hockey mask you're not exactly going to be making a sequel to *Titanic*. Start with what you know, and work with what's available to you. Doing every-possible-thing that you can do yourself without having to outsource to even your best friends will keep you going. The more money you save by doing it yourself, yet still get it out there in a way that you're proud of, will be the difference between one release and one hundred.

They say that you can't judge a book by its cover, but you're not going to buy *The White Album*, if it wasn't for the music inside. People need to see and feel and taste what they're buying, so the better you can make that release look the more likely it is to sell. Ultimately getting the band heard, this is why you're doing it right? So learn some graphic design software (there's even free ones online). If that's not your bag there's always spray paint and photocopiers, whatever it takes to stand out is what you're looking for. If you're completely inept artistically you can always beg a friend for assistance. These days everybody knows at least one person who has a copy of Photoshop.

Next it's important to remember to only put out bands that you're passionate about. You're not doing yourself or the band any favors by just putting them out. If you don't love the band, you're not going to be putting forth the right amount of effort. I get excited by the things I release, and that's because Thunder Bunny, Baby Birds Don't Drink Milk, Velma and the Happy Campers and Switchblade Cheetah might just be the most brilliant bands I've ever heard. Not to just single those guys out or sound too soap boxy, but it's just not worth the headache of putting all your energy into a project you just don't give a fuck about. This is where you should refer back to how much money you'll be making off your label...

probably nothing. That is unless it's a hip-hop label you're starting, just forget everything I said because that's where the money's at.

Edward Bignar of Workerbee Records, in the last year he has released more albums than Robert Pollard and has no social life. Does graphic design, works full time, is Rev. DeSade of The Cryogenic Strawberries and runs Workerbee Buttons (amongst other money making schemes) with his fiancé Emily without whom he wouldn't get anything done. He also swears he'll climb a tower with a rifle if Thunder Bunny doesn't win a Grammy in 2012.

Co-Operative Bliss
By Anja McCloskey

I will start this article in a truly straightforward fashion – running a co-operative record label is absolute madness and requires a never ending amount of patience, passion and benevolence. It is moments where I find myself standing in a function room, cluelessly holding a discarded bicycle wheel with long red and white ribbons attached to it and minutes before doors open, whilst an indefinite quantity of sketchy looking musicians carry boxes and instruments past me with no clear direction, that I ask myself, why I am doing this...

But then this mad collection of artists somehow manages to find structure in these chaotic patterns and everything always ends up being just fine. I am not sure how or why, but I have learnt to trust in this frenzied little network and, if I am honest, the friendships that we have built amongst each other are often assurance enough, that we will be okay.

Sotones Records is the UK's only co-operatively run record label. This means that the label is owned by the artists that are signed to it. Furthermore, we are registered as a not-for-profit Prozac Nation and use any revenue generated to develop our roster and to nurture new talent. It took the label a long time to get to this point. What started originally as a club night in 2004 organized by brothers Rob and Dave Wade-Brown in Southampton, a small city on England's South Coast, eventually merged into a co-operative in 2007.

What does it mean to collectively own a record label? Essentially it is pretty much chaos, but also a lot of ideas and collaboration. In essence, however much you invest into the organization is however much you get out of it. We hold annual general meetings to hire (and fire) our "staff", which are made up of artists, as well as volunteers and interns. Next to our Managing

Director, there are a number of other posts, such as Finance Director, A&R Director and Public Relations Liaison Officer, which have to be filled to ensure that there is at least a hint of structure in place.

Since its inception, Sotones has worked with nearly twenty artists and bands, including Band of Skulls (then known as Fleeingnewyork) and The Moulettes, and has set up distribution, publishing and marketing deals for its artists. Our signings have played across the UK and Europe and have supported acts, such as The Ting Tings, The Holloways and Noisettes and we have released over 25 records to date – an achievement that we are all very proud of.

My own band Haunted Stereo joined Sotones Records in November 2009 and the benefits we were able to draw from being a part of the label were immense and immediately felt. Being able to rely on the support of label mates and share all kinds of expertise, from marketing, to venue contacts, to recording skills, made us feel so much more connected. There is nothing more assuring than feeling that you are a part of something, especially if this something is a reliable network of skilled and compassionate musicians.

As artists, we retain all of the copyright for our work and license the material to Sotones Records for release. This way we maintain ownership of our ideas and recordings, but can, at the same time, draw upon the label's established processes, such as distribution and marketing. This has been hugely beneficial for us as a group. I remember spending hours stuffing envelopes with CDs and posting these out to publications, as well as being unsure in regards to making the most of digital publishing and filing claims for performance royalties. In a way Sotones Records has given us more autonomy as a band, as we can benefit from the power of the collective whilst still remaining truly individual.

I do not want to lie. Running a label in this manner – a collaborative network without a central office and a Managing Director without a mobile phone – can be very chaotic.

But it can also lead to truly beautiful moments. For example, after finally establishing how to fix the bicycle wheel and ribbons I was holding to the ceiling of the Old Queen's Head Pub in London, we were able to open the doors to our first London label showcase, celebrating 1313 days as a record label and the release of a sampler that was paid for entirely with revenue from record sales. The room was heaving and all of my label mates were there, watching each other perform to an energetic audience.

None of us would have been able to organize such an event on our own. It is only when we combine our talents that we are able to gather momentum, and that is exactly what Sotones Records is about – providing a platform and a network for independent artists to reach their audience and share their expertise with other musicians. Oh – and meet some of your best friends along the way!

Anja McCloskey is a half German, half American accordionist and singer songwriter currently residing in Southampton, England. As well as gigging and recording extensively with her band Haunted Stereo and her solo projects, she is also the Finance Director of Sotones Records, the UK's only co-operatively run not-for-profit record label. In her free time she enjoys writing for various music publications, such as Wears the Trousers Magazine.

Net Effects: Independent Music and the Internet
By Thom Carter

Without a doubt, the most influential music I have heard in the last 5 years has been from artists who self-release online. Period. Be they making classical music, alt-folk, pop, or just downright non-categorizing noise, they all share a common thread – literally, that of the cable that leads from their modem to the phone socket, and onwards into the great plains of internet-land.

Much has been said about the dilapidating effect that the Internet has had on the music business – and in terms of lost earnings from internet piracy and file-sharing, that is certainly true. But as a tool for independent musicians to gain exposure and an audience for their work, the Internet has been the driving force in a very positive revolution.

With the help of an explosion in the Net label scene (including online music journalism) and a plethora of high-quality, easy to use self-publishing platforms such as CD Baby and Bandcamp, a door has opened for musicians that are unique and genuinely unprecedented in the history of recorded sound. With the advent of powerful, relatively cheap computers and home-recording equipment, the landscape of self-publishing in music has changed beyond recognition, going from sweaty mixtapes of demos on cassette into one of highly professional, determined, and technologically literate artists who effectively function as their own shop front, PR and record label.

For that reason, a door has also opened for audiences too. For those with even the slightest inkling that they might be being hoodwinked by the mainstream media into travelling down a cultural cul-de-sac, finding and listening to independent artists' work online can be a real breath of fresh air. The Internet has made it possible to listen directly to music from the artist concerned, rather than to find out about bands only through the programming choices of radio DJs or the hyperbole of print magazine articles, which are too often skewed by commercialism and the cult of celebrity. I would go so far as to say that, in an age where what once was 'alternative' in fashion, music and art has now become just another branch of conformity to be successfully marketed to a target audience of open mouths and open wallets. (Think of the 'Rage Against the Machine vs. The X-Factor chart battle over Christmas 09, where both acts were presented as being the antithesis of each other but are in fact signed to the same Major Label –Sony BMG) The internet and the artists using it appear to be almost the only credible, authentic cultural movement of the era.

The net-audio scene has already produced some absolute gems – investigate the music of the Dutch band The Black Atlantic, for instance, or the classical music of Spanish artist Bosques di me Mente, or German singer/songwriter Julia Kotowski's folk songs as Entertainment for the Braindead – all of whom have gained international exposure and acclaim for their work from having utilised the potential of the internet and self-marketing.

Perhaps the most interesting recent case-study of a musician self-publishing online is the Ukulele-strumming songstress and Brighton resident Sophie Madeline. Her album *Love, Life, Ukulele* (entirely self-produced) was re-packaged with more attractive cover art and re-released as a limited-edition vinyl (with digital download included on purchase) as the first physical release on the excellent, newly founded Bandcamp-offshoot, Bandcamp Wax. The song-writing and production are superb – proving once again that artists armed with little more than their wits, a laptop and a microphone can make studio-quality records any day of the week – and the edition of 500 records (at $25 each) sold out very quickly. Her music has since been licensed for use on numerous adverts and television shows, and as far as I know, she is operating completely on her own, without any record label support except for the small monetary investment from the people at Bandcamp in pressing her album onto vinyl.

I doubt very much if any of the above acts, and so many others like them, would have seen the light of day prior to the Internet. They are each unique: so idiosyncratic, so unpredictable, that it is almost inconceivable to think that they would have made such beautiful, warm, personal recordings had they been squeezed and shaped to fit the conventional formulas of the music business and the studio recording process. However – it is interesting to note that large independent labels are now starting to use the self-same platforms to promote and distribute their music as unsigned artists have been using all along. For the release of well-established indie star Sufjan Stevens' new EP, *All Delighted People*, his label, Asthmatic Kitty, chose to make the album available only on Bandcamp for 3 days before it hit other digital stores. The experiment was an out-and-out success, with over 10,000 copies sold in a single weekend and the EP debuting high in the Billboard Charts. In an interview with Bandcamp founder Ethan Diamond, John Beeler of Asthmatic Kitty said of the labels promotional effort:

"We sent it out first to our mailing list; they tend to be our most informed and dedicated fans. Shortly after sending the email we posted it as a news item to our site, then tweeted it, then ran it on Facebook".

Now, I'm sure Asthmatic Kitty also has a promotional budget for advertising and a seriously long list of media contacts that they sent that email out to as well, but other than that, there is simply no difference in his actual strategy than that of pretty much any other band trying to get attention for its latest release online. Other than posing the question 'why does Sufjan Stevens need a label at all now he has a large fan base and an email account?', the above example only goes to show how much the gap between what signed and unsigned artists can do with their music has diminished with the rise of internet self-publishing tools. If even large commercial labels are using Facebook and Bandcamp as their first choice means to connect with audiences and sell and promote music, then that gap has become very small indeed.

So, what for the future? Well, I think that the culture of buying music is shifting in two ways. Firstly, it is clear that more and more people globally are buying music in digital form each year, and that CD sales are decreasing as a result. It doesn't mean that CDs will disappear, as people like to have a physical edition of something in their hands, but it does signal that there is a growing sense of trust in purchasing music online.

Secondly, I think that there is a growing realization amongst audiences that music piracy is essentially no different from shoplifting a CD, and is a huge problem for artists – most of whom are not earning a great deal from their recordings. Aside from the obvious need for lawmakers and Internet providers to get their act together and deal with online piracy, it is clear to me that there is already an audience-led change that is happening. Similar to the idea of Fair Trade for coffee growers and the like, a culture of consumer-led consciousness is becoming apparent in music. People appreciate that the 'grower' is an essential part of the chain, and many people downloading music online often even 'tip' the artist and pay more than the lowest recommended price when services like Bandcamp offer a 'pay what you want' model.

In an age where most bands have simply become their own label and learnt not only to record their own music but to book their own tours and print their own merchandise themselves, a wealth of well-produced, meaningful music is being made and released entirely independently. Most importantly, it is being heard. The state of play now is not so much a question of those who are Signed and those who are invisible, but of those who are Signed, and those who simply sign themselves.

Thom Carter is a multi-instrumentalist musician and producer from Oxford, England. He has collaborated with a number of musicians internationally and released his own solo albums under various different artist names). In 2009, he co-founded the commercial label Verlaine Records, and when not in the studio, he is a keen cyclist, beachcomber and photographer.

On Scenes and Valleys: What We Learned in the '90s and Who We Are Now

By Giacomo Bottà

On my bedside table I have a copy of *Manchester. Looking at the Light From the Pouring Rain*, a photo book by Kevin Cummins. Cummins is a Manchester born photographer, who worked for the British magazine NME for many years. He had the chance to document and in a way forge visually the Manchester scene, i.e. one of the first scenes around the world where independent music played a significant role. I guess that if I say Buzzcocks, Joy Division, The Fall, The Smiths, you all know what I am talking about.

I think this is the most important point: independent music is linked to scenes. Without scenes, there would be no independent music and vice versa. Let me get there by referring to my own little independent world.

My own little independent world happened in the last decade of the previous century, in an alpine valley in the very north of Italy, on the border with Switzerland (that's in central Europe). Italy is the place where pizza comes from, while Switzerland, the one where cuckoo clocks come from. Imagine coming from a place between the two.

Anyway, this valley cuts the Alps longitudinally and people tend to live in the bottom of it, along a river and a kind of narrow motorway, which connects towns and villages. The closest metropolis is Milan, the world capital of fashion, and you could get there after riding a slow train or a car through endless tunnels, along a lake. Anyway, you tend not to go to Milan very often, once in a while, for a gig that you cannot miss, save the fact that any of you have a driving license.

Back in the day, all the local infrastructures related to music making were in the hands of semi-professional/amateur disco or rock musicians. They owned small studios, sold overpriced second-hand instruments, rented out Pas, knew how to handle a mixing desk or an effect rack and sometimes published records with their own small labels, which were 'independent', but as greedy and gain-driven as the worst majors.

In my own little independent world, we bought records from obscure Xeroxed mailing lists or at gigs, we wrote letters to Dischord asking if Fugazi would play in our town (Fugazi always answered, they are the kindest band in music history) and we were demanding community spaces for our own self-organized gigs.

The independent bands of the 1990s in the valley learnt how to put out DIY cassettes and later CDs along the years. Some labels were created for that purpose and some individuals started taking care exclusively of that, building networks a bit all around the world, exchanging materials and helping bands in getting gigs or setting up tours. It was very exciting to see a local band featured on a cassette sample released in South America or reviewed on a fanzine from Asia. It was within these confirmations that we existed.

We understood ourselves as a scene. Being a scene was fun. We met, chatted and laughed, we rehearsed, discussed, fantasized about and produced music the way we wanted. We were also envious of each other's 'success', fought, couldn't get things done, went chaotic, stole money, drank too much, talked hypocritically, decided arbitrarily what was independent (alternative, antagonist, against-the-system…) and what not, we were lazy and set too high of moral standards, that we were breaking all the time. We were truly independent.

Then, at a certain point, the internet came. That should have meant more connections, more exchanges and more music to share and produce. It also became easy to record or design a poster or promote a band in distant places. That also meant that it was not so important anymore from which scene of which you came from. It became more important which genre, as defined by MySpace, you were into. The big enemies, the major labels, also started having some problems and nowadays they seem not to have a clue.

So, independent music today, huh? Independent music for me is still a great means to get to know wonderful people. I rarely met someone involved with it that was an asshole. It is also the only way I want to get my own music out. I want people to listen to my music and be able to say: I can do it too! (And then do it). It is also the only music I still like to listen to and to pay for. And it is the only music where you can still get that feeling of belonging to a scene, though scattered and loose.

One of the records we all loved back then was *Warehouse: Songs and Stories* by a band from Minneapolis called Hüsker Dü. In the inlay notes of that record there were THE words. THE words are: *Revolution starts at home. Preferably in the bathroom mirror.* That is independent music: a way to get to do things at home in a revolutionary way and a revolutionary way to get to know yourself.

Giacomo Bottà *is a part-time punk, full-time daddy and holds a PhD in cultural studies, which allows him to lecture and research about popular music scenes. He has just released an EP as Jaakko, which you can download for free at the We Were Never Being Boring Collective's blog. He currently lives in Strasbourg, France and occasionally spends time in the bathroom mirror, but then shakes his head and goes back to work.*

The Good Madness
By Roberto Vodanovic

I am a baldheaded, furious, self declared poet.
My guitar is out of tune, my singing is out of tune too.
I am happy, I am sad, I have a handful of tears for everybody.
All I need is my guitar, three chords, a couple of verses, all I need is
love, all I need I already have.
I was born once. I don't remember it. I will die one day, they say,
but I don't think about that.
Meanwhile, I live the way I want to and the way I need to.
I draw comics because they amuse me,
I paint because it relaxes me.
I do music. I write verses because I have to. They just appear from
nowhere. I have to throw them on the paper.

Sometimes it is very pleasant experience, like making love.
Sometimes it is a torture, like vomiting.
Either way it is a catharsis. I weep my verses, I bleed them and
scream.
I am taking you for a journey, you just observe.
You will see the same but different.
I don't consent to The Imitation of Life, I dream only about The
Great Escape.
 I am looking at the world as The Bunch of Pictures with my Glass
Eyes of a Clown.
I tell my story about The Good Madness.
Brlog Records (Brlog meaning a den – animal shelter, a lair) is my
sanctuary and my friends' sanctuary as well.

We call ourselves The New Outlaws.
I'm damned if I agree, and dead, if I give up.
Endless Strange Journey Begins Again.

The World Should Listen to What We Have To Say: Being an Independent Musician of the Third World

By Justinus Irwin

The clock was showing 07.47 PM and I was alone at JIST, a dingy music studio that costs us not more than USD 5$ per two hours. The rehearsal was supposed to start at 8 PM and, unfortunately, there was an album to finish in such a short deadline. I was sitting alone on a bench, waiting for Wahyu "Acum" Nugroho, the singer and bass player, and also Dedyk Eryanto who plays drum for the band. 45 minutes later they came without saying anything. The weary faces, wet clothes and grin of despair. It was an unpleasant experience, but we could not say anything to each other. In silence we were entering the studio, trying to have a decent rehearsal with the remaining time. What more to say? We have day jobs to maintain and we need the money to maintain our music. We furiously cursed Jakarta for what happened. The most crowded city in Indonesia. Just a glimpse of our routine.

Being independent musician in Indonesia means having two different professions in a day. If playing music is considered as night job, then day job is a must for any independent musician. Yes, a day job that has nothing to do with playing music. Much like being a teacher, book editor, journalist, lawyer, general practician or any profession that produces good money. Seemingly, Indonesia turns out to be a wrong choice for picking a career in independent music. Like many other countries of the third world, Indonesia is always busy struggling with poverty and economic issues, and is clearly unready for a "revolution" in its music industry. The boys and I have been in an independent band, Bangkutaman, for more than 10 years now and, clearly, certain values can be shared. Values that are manifested from many great experiences. This is not America, this is not England, This is Indonesia!

This is Indonesia!

It is probably unwise if "rupiah" is the main reason of playing independent music in Indonesia. The story might be different if your band already belongs to the major labels. Unfortunately, every good musician has to start from zero point: being independent and trying to get a good record deal. From my perspective, market determines the music and not the other way around. This is clearly a mistake. You are just making crappy songs and you are not being honest to yourself, and of course, your music. It is a shame. Being honest to your music is crucial. It should be liberating, and you can play anything you want for the rest of your life.

However, everything is possible in Indonesia if efforts are done hard enough. By effort, I mean an exhausting and depressing struggle. Other than hard work, strong self-confidence is essential. Strong self-confidence is different from being arrogant though. Again, if you are thinking about independent music, the first thing that should come to your mind is neither money nor popularity. In contrary, it should be networking! Now when you hear a word such as "networking", you might think of a business plan. Well, it does not have to be that way all the time. The term networking here means building quality communication with almost everybody you meet. Always mingle with new and potential crowd, which is about it. Do not ever thinking about using drugs or consuming too much alcohol like a conventional life style of rock stars. You need to keep it sober, remember: you have day job to maintain.

D.I.Y. Attitude

Your attitude determines the success. The right attitude is a must, and it is definitely not doing the conventional rock star attitude either. This is Indonesia! Of course, a conventional work ethic still plays an important role here, to include discipline, responsibility, integration, good communication, and never giving up. But the key is not to be a spoiled musician. Be independent! Do not ever think you are the best musician in the world with phenomenal songs that people would certainly love in an instant. In contrary, think of yourself as "nothing." Embrace the Do-It-Yourself (DIY) culture to achieve the goals. Just do your best in albums and live performances, and consider success or popularity as a bonus. Get out from your comfort zone and challenge yourself with a brand new level of experience. This is the best part if you are up for greatest moment in musical career. The memories will always remain. The good ones!

Bangkutaman & Ian Brown

Acum talked to Ian Brown a month ago in Bali. The living legend. The godlike genius. Former singer of the phenomenal band from Manchester, The Stone Roses. Acum, who is also a music journalist, was supposed to interview the "king monkey" actually, but Ian found out that Acum was a great accompany. So they talked some more rather than having a standard interview. As Acum had told me, Ian Brown adores the punk attitude. *"The Sex Pistols taught us well. You don't have to be great singer or guitar player just to be in a band. Be true to yourself and the world will notice your existence,"* said Acum imitating Ian Brown. If The Sex Pistols taught something important to Ian Brown, well, The Stone Roses taught us [Bangkutaman] something important too.

This is why the self-titled album of The Stone Roses means so much more than just a great album to us all. We find the energy. We find the essence. We find the art. We find the glory. We adore The Stone Roses for those things. Yes, we have been waiting for roughly 10 years just to see Ian Brown performed on stage in Jakarta, Indonesia. You know, The Stone Roses were not "available" anymore after 1996, so watching Ian Brown in live version was a stunning and nearly magical experience for Bangkutaman. This is one of the special bonuses for the hard work me and the boys have done. We were able to Witness Ian Brown wearing a Bangkutaman t-shirt, as well as personally receiving our latest album, *Ode Buat Kota*.

Make A Better Life Through Independent Music

It is a blunder to accuse the government for your failure in a musical career. Stop blaming others just to make your own self feel better. Blaming others will not solve any problems. It would be so much nicer if you try to adapt with every single circumstance. Especially the horrible ones. Have a good faith in your music. So, if you are playing music for fun, keep it fun then. But if you are playing music for life, keep it serious! Or, in my opinion, the best combination probably is to have a serious and fun career in independent music. Ask yourself now! Until this very moment, we still challenge ourselves with extraordinary things. We may not produce a good sum of money from the band (for now), but our day jobs provide it all. We have family and own place to live. Everything is in balance because we do not just do music, but we are the music.

Justinus Irwin is a guitarist/song writer for Indonesian folk rock/indie pop band, Bangkutaman, and editor-in-chief of Campus Indonesia magazine. He is also acts as a freelance writer and book editor. More importantly, he is a faithful husband who loves entrepreneurship. Bangkutaman has just released their album, Ode Buat Kota, which available through mail order.

Of Max Martin: The Social Psychology of Band Break-Ups

By David Redmalm

I believe many of you are uncomfortably familiar with Britney Spears' neotenized pez- and Prozac-popping Muzak, as well as Bon Jovi's sexless cock-rock. Many of you are also probably aware that the Swedish producer Max Martin (real name Martin Karl Sandberg) has worked with both of them – he has also written and produced songs for Backstreet Boys, Kelly Clarkson, Kate Perry and Pink. Wow, what a CV.

People who care about music in Sweden – creative and visionary people working with music full-time or part-time, or at night-time and during weekends, with the ambition to put their souls into creating something ear-provoking, inspiring, emotionally rich and utterly unique – wish that Sweden would be first and foremost known for talents such as The Knife, The Soundtrack of Our Lives, Promise and the Monster and Dungeon, but the fact is that it's the mainstream producers, together with the endless releases and re-releases of ABBA compilations, that has made Sweden into one of the largest music exporters in the world.

I really don't like Max Martin. It's nothing personal. I've never met him, or even heard him say anything in an interview, but for me, somehow and for some reason, he has become a symbol for the commoditization of music – a danger to the creativity of the music scene. I've been engaged in several non commercial, alternative music projects, some alternative to the extent that they hardly even existed. In my creative work as an unpaid amateur musician, Max Martin – the myth, the symbol, the trope – has thus been an important source of aggressive energy.

I've made myself inversely dependent of Max Martin. Me and my fellow musicians in the various constellations I was a part of in my adolescent years continuously referred both explicitly and implicitly to Max Martin and his likes during our heated discussions in the rehearsal room. I think that the French philosopher Jaques Derrida can be of help in understanding this aspect of my identity as a musician. He has argued that every categorization is always a matter of postponing the question of what the categorized thing really is. To put it more clearly: When I ask myself "Who am I" there are a lot of answers to that question, and some of the answers are probably even mutually exclusive. There is no straight answer, so the only way to deal with the question is to postpone the actual answer by defining myself in terms of what I'm *not*. And for example, when writing music and playing gigs, I'm not commercial, not a sell-out (obviously, since I hardly make any money out of my music). I am not Max Martin.

Dissociating oneself from Max Martin was of course very important for the members of the band I played with as a teenager. We were named Lemur, after Jean-Paul Sartre's short story and the Strepsirrhini primate (I know, the pun is pretty lame). We were inspired by free jazz, post-rock, chamber pop and Swedish straight edge hardcore. Sounds great? Well, you haven't heard any of our CD-Rs, have you? We did everything to 'stay true to our ideals,' as we said, which meant that we tried as hard as possible to avoid making people like us.

I remember that at the only gig we actually got paid for doing, we decided to randomly tune each other's instruments before the show and improvise the whole gig, finding out one's tuning while playing (we agreed that the fact that they wanted to pay us was an insult to our artistic integrity). I also remember that we were always late for the rehearsals, sometimes even an hour (except for the poor, punctual saxophonist). We recorded our demos ourselves on primitive equipment that we couldn't manage instead of using our summer job salaries to buy time in the local music studio, which was really cheap. We wanted to be completely DIY, but we didn't really do it ourselves, since the result bore the stamp of our profound incompetence. When we for once wrote a beautiful ballad, we decided to interrupt the song with an atonal cacophony, played by a saxophone and a trumpet, accompanied by a sampled and deconstructed avant-jazz drum solo. One of our songs could have as much as 6 changes in rhythm. One of the catchiest tunes we ever wrote – a bit of John McEntireish drums, a bit of 80's Casio synthesizer, a steady bass riff and intense guitar plucking – was pitched down to half the speed before we put it on a CD since our drummer would quit the band otherwise. As you can see, we did everything in our power to *not* become successful.

My girlfriend studied social psychology at the time and had an assignment where she was supposed to study group behavior. She and a couple of her classmates came to observe one of our rehearsals and interviewed each member of the band separately. Their diagnosis: the band was to break up within a year. There was no proper structure to the group, the members didn't perceive their roles in the group as meaningful, there were no common aims and there was a serious lack of mutual respect.

And you know what? They were right. About a year after the study was carried out, the band members went separate ways. The drummer had quit playing drums and wanted to take music to strange new places with the software synthesizers he had installed on his second hand PC. The guitarist hated to rehearse – "Why play the same song twice?" he asked. Personally, I was kind of tired of the whole thing and wanted to play indie pop instead. The saxophonist started studying music at the university – he's now the only one of us who works with music full-time. Apparently, we should have listened more to him, and we shouldn't have let him wait for us an hour before every rehearsal, especially not during winter, which can be quite harsh in Sweden. My girlfriend, by the way, is soon taking her PhD in social psychology.

An unvigilant reader may come to the conclusion that this text is a vindication for mainstream music. But I'd like to end this text by repeating the argument that Max Martin's bad attitude is killing the creativity in the music business. We must persist in the critique of the commoditization of art, because it empties aesthetics of its meaning and it bereaves the artist of her/his soul. But I cannot get rid of the nagging feeling that Lemur could have become so much more if its members would've focused less on not being sell-outs, and more on writing good music. Indie music and DIY music means being independent of – and doing things without the help of – people like Max Martin. But you're not really independent of these people if you constantly define yourself in opposition to them. We – the members of Lemur – had our minds set on being in opposition to everything lucrative; what if we instead had set our minds on creating something ear-provoking, inspiring, emotionally rich and utterly unique, in itself and of itself?

David Redmalm makes music under his family name. He is a PhD student in sociology at Örebro University, Sweden, and writes about the pet phenomenon and its implications for contemporary society and social theory, with a special interest in Paris Hilton's Chihuahua Tinkerbell. Songs by Redmalm has been released by Series Two Records (USA) and the Swedish labels Friendly Noise.

An Arrangement of Scattered Memories, Feelings, Beats
By Christopher Eaves

Humanity is unique in possessing one characteristic over all other life. Humanity possesses the sole ability of understanding the idea of having a future, of looking past the needs of the now, the needs of hunger, reproduction, and shelter in order to build toward a future rather than forced to react to the demands of the present. Humanity builds culture as it progresses forward growing its understanding of this universe, although sometimes physically violent through war, sometimes physically peaceful through art and music, but in either case always due to the gift and responsibility of understanding the concept of having a future to work towards. Culture is the sum of all humanities' experiences. The future is understood by the past encounters we all commutatively have lived through and learned from. Memories are created through us, through our actions and interaction, by both the great and the terrible occurrence alike, as it is to be human it is to be a part of humanity as we are all defined by these experiences and memories we create together over time which flows from our lone understanding of such an idea. These memories are shaped and influenced by all other experiences we have obtained forming an always expanding narrative of living as we are the universe's creators' of feelings, creators' of understanding, creators' of music, and creators' of memories.

The once upon a time of my life is a collection of scattered thoughts islanded in a sea of stars, cut, folded, and arranged within each other forming a single narrative in the way a dream may feel in the first few moments of an awakened confused morning consciousness. These once detached and autonomous stories now blend together forming a single life event of memory. Was the show in December, or was it back in July? What was the weather like? I remember rain, or at least I remember I brought a coat, I think, right? Was it at the dive bar up on the north side, or did they play down Main Street at the Vine? Perspective of remembering is reality in that the feelings that those memories create are true to the individual. Memories now joined together is the base for seeing and understanding the future, for helping to decide my likes, determining why I have a taste for a genre of music, and forming the foundation of character.

Mistakes are one of the most important parts of life. They're underrated and most people seem to avoid making them at all costs, afraid of them. These are not things that need to be feared but rather fought for and pursued as mistakes teach us and give understanding. They are much a part of the human condition as breathing. For myself such a time came when I challenged my parents' control in the midst of youth self discovery and personal awareness. I did not stay (as a standard cliché) home and study for a chemistry exam the next day, although the exact night of week eludes my memory a decade later. There where consequences for my actions but they are not important, they were short term problems for a person with the gift of being a species with long term foresight. I left home giving my parents the impression I was going to go study at my friend's house but instead attended my first live music show, to find a place in my developing character for the listening and feelings of an emotional and personal experience to which music offers our society. A portion of my developing character was born that unknowing night like so many other people that age, an experience which I still carry with me.

One of the few places to see a local show in a small less then socially accepting town was a place known as the Vine, featuring what could only be defined by the broadest of definitions a small stage with green glow paint tucked away in the front corner of the building next to the entrance. The place has been shut down for more than a decade now, although twenty more such places have sprung up in its place over the years, one by one, to only have shut down themselves after a time – this is the nature of the local venue of small towns I think. The room is loud as a mixed tape plays over the Frankenstein audio set up, everyone is yelling to talk but no one is louder than anyone else. A second floor with old secondhand couches (it was always dark, I choose not to think about what light would reveal) overlooked the stage and lower standing area – a good place to take a girl to make out and make new mistakes and new experiences. For some reason next to the couches were torn up boxes of Monopoly and Stratego board games with missing pieces, I never understood why. The venue was dark to the point it was hard to walk around without slamming into someone, a wall, or a chair. Routinely a PBR would roll out of band member's backpack while bringing the equipment in through the cramped front door. The music goers were scattered around the walls, sitting on tables, and window ledges, conversing with each other as the band setup their equipment – this could take five minutes or an hour but most never really cared. A guitar riff cuts through the air seemingly out of nowhere and everywhere, bouncing off all the walls – the acoustics where at least good. All conversations ended simultaneously throughout the room as in unison everyone turned towards the front stage as the band began to play. The two and half working stage lights turned on revealing the band on stage, appearing to be more than men in the moment, local rock stars. Music began to flow from the stage, overflowing the space. This was my first experience with the world of independent music, as I attempt to recall the event the best I can. I know not all of these memories come from the same experience but they are now all attached and interwoven together in the same narrative and feeling.

So it is here that I must say I have never written a piece of music, I don't make music, I can't read music, I've never attended a music class, I can barely keep a beat on the drums. I composed a seven track album once upon a time in an altered state within a foggy white smoke euphoria surrounded by smiling friends. I used a fifty dollar program picked up and purchased from a big box store shelf; one aisle up from the craft supplies and one aisle over from kitchen gadgetry – mostly samples with a digital mixer. My number one song was called Guns, and I was known as Sir Isaac Newton's Gravity Attack.

This is the tale of my first independent music experience as I had shared it with many great people. We shared this experience and we carry this time within each of us. My memories, once separate and easily distinguishable from each other are now intermixed to the point it's impossible to know which memory belonged to which events, to which show, or to which show's after party, but this doesn't matter as the feelings of these experiences, interactions and conversations with those people in those times, the personal feelings of the music in the air, to have actually felt the air move from the speaker drivers for the very first time represent the ideas of humanity through the experience of music. The exact dates of these events don't matter, but the fact that I experienced them dose; it was true and I felt it, and continue to feel it when I place a CD in the tray or turn my iPod on. These memories began my love for listening to music, which I feel so many people also carry with them and experience every day. The story continuing on into tomorrow's future by all of us, moving forward into the next music event adding the cumulative experience into our shared humanity. What does all of this mean, in the grand scheme of life and metaphor? It means nothing and it means everything.

Christopher Eaves *is a writer and director/screenwriter living in Vancouver, Washington. He has directed and written several web series and is currently working on developing his first full length feature film. He is also working on creating 40 short screenplays in 52 weeks through his own company, 40 in 52 productions.*

Breaking Down "Indie"
By Tim Chaplin & Christina Marie

Indie's a funny word. I used to think it meant stuff like The Smiths and The House Of Love – not really my cup of tea at all. Then I caught on to the idea of indie as independent. Now, *that's* much more like it. Doing things for yourself – in some cases, often by yourself, out of sheer necessity – or just because you want to. And answering to no one. That's got much more in common with the punk aesthetic than dour, grey stuff.

I had a friend for whom the term indie was an insult. Even if referring to it in the independent sense, as opposed to the more musical pigeonhole. He may well have turned his nose up at the limiting, self-defeatist attitude. The shying away from any mainstream success, if you like. Nothing wrong with trying to be a rock 'n' roll star, you understand. And indeed he was.

So, indie and independent, is it really the same thing? Well, maybe. I think it is fine to give a name to your approach and outlook. A name for actual sounds and songs seems much less necessary though. Who really has any right to do that? I find music very hard to describe. It means different things to different people. No one's right and no one is wrong. You can't tell someone *how* to listen. Actually, I'm sure some people have tried, but that's just silly. So, music's for listening to and not writing about. Everyone knows that. Okay, but what the fuck am I doing right now, then? Why do we read stacks of music magazines and blogs? Eager and avid to know what someone else tells us about the way they think something might sound?

Music is very important to me. Listening to it and making it as a fan and as a musician. Am I an indie artist? Don't know – you tell me. I get called it often enough – in terms of the way some of my music sounds and even in terms of the way I look. I don't mind one bit. It's interesting to hear what people think what I do might be. I sure as hell don't know. It is what it is. What I *do* know, is that I often operate independently. So… fair enough.

A new project I have been concentrating on recently is Factory Kids – a duo with Christina Marie. We think we're a pop band. At least I *think* we think we are. It was suggested we might try to address any gender issues here that we may or may not have encountered. We had a quick think and could not remember a single one. Maybe our spiritual predecessors - if we're even *allowed* to associate ourselves with their hallowed output – might say differently. The Vaselines, Royal Trux and Joy Zipper may well have had to put in some of the groundwork. I don't see why, but anyway. Christina might touch upon this some more in her half of this thing…

Right, all that remains is for me to remind you to keep listening and to keep making noise. It does not have to have a name, but, if it must, indie's just as good as any other.

-Tim Chaplin

Agreeing with Tim, indie has been a funny word, relating to a certain genre of music. However, when using this word in the past to describe a sound for a band that has a sound similar to that of The Smiths or Primal Scream, but considering The Smiths and Primal Scream released their albums in the US through Warner Bros., that is hardly "indie". So, what can be described as "indie" is a band who releases music through an independent label, but that includes many different genres of music.

Indie can also be a dirty word. In the past, I have known people in the London music scene that shunned the use of the word indie in any capacity when relating to a band. However, these same people also shunned any bands that were hyped-up or achieved fame and success. It is a funny thing, isn't it? It seems like the only people who received credibility were the ones who did almost everything themselves or were signed to a small (but not indie!) label with a solid, but not too big, following.

In regards to gender relations within what some call indie music scenes, I am fortunate enough to have never really experienced discrimination due to my gender. Sure, I have had disagreements and have been disrespected by band mates, but that happens regardless of gender. I have a friend who is now a New York "indie" celebrity, but during her humble beginnings of playing small venues, a major record label representative wanted to sign her band – without her, even though she wrote all the songs and has the most powerful voice out there. What's the reason for this? Because her image was not the one they wanted. Rather, they were looking for a "Jessica Simpson type" to front the band. Well, the deal didn't happen, but it always struck a chord with me. Both her and I agreed that the situation would not have happened if she was a guy. I think women, regardless of their appearance, can be successful. However, there are still superficial standards that women must fit into in order to achieve mainstream "indie" success.

My project of the past two years has been Factory Kids, with Tim Chaplin. People seem to compare us to The Raveonettes, The Kills, Royal Trux, even the Ting Tings! I think people just see a guy/girl duo and group them into a category with other guy/girl duos, even if there music isn't at all similar. Not only with guy/girl duos but I still find that if there is a band with girls in it, they can be called a term I loathe, "chick band" , even if there are guys in the band! I think that is proof that despite all the female musicians who have achieved success in recent years, women still have a long way to go when it comes to what most call "indie" music. Unfortunately the music business is still male-dominated and it can only be a matter of time until things will continue to get better.

-Christina Marie

Tim Chaplin is a musician, songwriter, producer and remixer. Working under his own name for song based material and the Luminous alias for more electronic/experimental sounds. Tim is also one half of the band Factory Kids.

Christina Marie is a musician and painter. She is a former member of New York shoegaze bands The Modern Hour and Audn. Christina is also one half of the band Factory Kids.

Who Stole My Indie?
By Jon E. Hardy

When I was first approached to write a piece for this book about independent music and its influence on me, I really didn't know what to write. And As I sit down to begin, I still don't!

I'm always very wary and uncomfortable talking about myself and my music as it's easy to cross the line into self-indulgence or just sounding plain pompous, arrogant or me, me, me about things. But, as this is supposed to be about my own opinions & feelings, let's see how things go.

PART I – DISCOVERY

I first discovered the independent music scene when I was around 15-16 at school. Bored of chart music and a little lost for where to turn next, but as yet unable to play any instrument myself (I don't come from a musical family, nobody can read or play music, and family members aren't too interested on the whole).

I think it was a gradual awakening rather than a sudden revelation – looking backwards to look forwards. Discovering and swapping records by The Who, The Jam, The Clash, Sex Pistols etc. This was before The Smiths came along and changed everything. It's funny now thinking back. When I was a teenager, we used to judge people purely by whether they liked The Smiths or not. That was the standard. If they didn't, they were out.

The very first time I met Richard who played in various bands with me over the years (including *The Pristines*), I can still remember the conversation. We met at Coventry Polytechnic, a friend I met there, Carl (who was also in our first band together), told me to talk to his friend from school, Richard, in a lecture we were both in (Carl not).

Me: *You're Richard aren't you? Carl's friend?*
Richard: *Yeah, are you Jon then? Do you like The Smiths?*

Me: *Of course. Everyone should shouldn't they?*
Richard: *Sit down then.*

But, that encounter was later. I was into my indie music and John Peel etc. by then. I was discovered not discovering.

There are 2 things I want to talk about as being important to me in my initial discovery of the independent music world:

Firstly, hearing *Hatful Of Hollow* by The Smiths for the first time when a school friend brought it over to play to me (he did try and persuade me of the virtues of the first Culture Club album at the same time, but I wasn't having it!). I adored *Hatful Of Hollow* and remember wanting to play guitar like Johnny Marr (still trying 20 years later) and write lyrics as profound, witty and moving as Morrissey (still trying 20 years later).

Secondly, was seeing a *South Bank Show* on a group called The Velvet Underground.

For those of you that don't know, the *South Bank Show* was a long running arts review show profiling artistes from the worlds of music, art, dance, literature etc. Of course, I was aware of Andy Warhol, Lou Reed, John Cale and Nico individually as artist, solo performer(s), producer, model etc. But, I had never heard of The Velvet Underground. You have to remember this was before the days of the internet or multi-channel TV, so media & information was not as readily available as today.

I was mesmerized by this band. How cool they looked. Their unique sound. I thought "Venus In Furs" was the greatest song I'd ever heard (The song still never fails to make the hairs on the back of my neck stand up even today). I recognized other songs from films – "Waiting For The Man", "Heroin". Or from other performer's versions – "All Tomorrow's Parties" (Japan), "White Light/White Heat" (Bowie – Ziggy incarnation era). I immediately asked for the complete album box set release (reissued in conjunction with the show) for my 16th birthday.

Now, with The Smiths and The Velvet Underground in my record collection, I knew I had truly discovered my kind of music. As my quest continued with the music press assistance, and unlikely source came to be one of, if not the biggest influence on myself and many of my generation. Radio. Radio purely in the guise of *John Peel* on late night BBC Radio 1.

I never bothered with Radio 1 much. It was, much like today, all about DJ personalities – Dave Lee Travis, Gary Davies, Tony Blackburn etc. who had no interest in the music they were playing and as far as they were concerned the show was all about them. Worst of all of these was *Steve Wright In The Afternoon* with his endless self-indulgent chatter and puerile comedy characters. Of course, sadly, these shows were hugely popular!

But, tucked away in a 10 p.m. – Midnight slot, in a dark corner of Broadcasting House was Mr. John Peel. Playing anything from punk, hardcore, hip-hop, trance, to country, rock'n'roll classics, reggae, dub and indie jangle. Nothing was off-limit (except the predictable and banal). In a time when Stock, Aitken & Waterman ruled the charts with their manufactured pop conveyer-belt, John Peel was a blessing to so many. It seems pointless to list all the bands I first heard on this show. Suffice to say, almost everyone of importance to me from that era. But, really, can you imagine hearing the likes of Peel favorites like The Fall or Bogshed anywhere else? So many great bands would have just been sadly lost, unheard and unrecorded forever, and so many mavericks & unheralded geniuses undiscovered.

I never understood the public outpouring of grief at the loss of royalty or a celebrity. It somehow sometimes seems an over-reaction. Of course it's sad, but are they really that much more important than other people who die, sometimes heroically – soldiers, firemen, rescue workers, etc. The prime example of this to me was Lady Diana. I thought, "These people don't know her; they've never met her. Why are they crying?" Why are they so sad about a stranger's death?

I never got it until the day John Peel died.

I'd grown up listening to him. He was such a genuine, unassuming, down-to-earth character. For him it was all about the music. He shunned the limelight and always seemed uncomfortable or embarrassed when it was forced upon him. Nobody had a bad word to say about the man. The tributes were many and moving. We will all be eternally grateful for what he gave us in our lives.

I was told that he played The Pristines' first single on his show once, by somebody that had heard it. I, sadly, did not hear it and it's something I will always regret. I can't explain how much it would have meant to me to hear him play it, and how proud and honoured it would have made me.

PART II – PARTICIPATION

For part one of my piece I wrote about my self-discovery of the independent music scene. For the second part I will endeavor to tell the story of my minor participations & contributions to the scene.

We formed our first band in Poly. It was more of a gang in those days – we rarely rehearsed all at the same time, and when we did we just made a huge old racket as we couldn't really play, but still wanted to sound like an early Jesus and Mary Chain. Can you imagine the cacophony?

I started playing tambourine, partly as homage to Martin St.John who did the same in Primal Scream at the time, and partly as I couldn't play anything else but was learning guitar off the two people in the band who knew about chords and all that tricky kind of stuff. I started to write songs, each one incorporating new chords as I learnt them. My first song was called Ashamed and was just *A*, *E* and *D*. By the next song I'd also learnt how to play a *G* so that was in there. Then a *C*. Then a *Am*. But *F* was always really hard then, As well as *B*. So, no *F's* or *B's* then! We were called The Puppets (after murderer Myra Hindley's dog rather tastelessly), and did one gig, well, I say gig – we played at a house party once. The guests listened to one song then disappeared into various other parts of the house or garden by midway through the second one. As did various members of the band as the "set" went on.

51

Still, by the next band, The Balloon Farm, it had improved. No, not the 1960's garage/Nuggets band by the same name. I'm not THAT old! We actually recorded properly with this band. This would be my first time in a real recording studio. We did one 3-track demo called *Apathy E.P* that was released as a 7" single (in Germany), a cassette single (in Spain), and a track from it on a flexi (in USA). Yeah, we really milked a lot of mileage from those 3 songs.

I have a lot of funny stories from The Balloon Farm days. Despite an almost Mark.E.Smith's *Fall-esque* number of members coming and going or participating over the couple of years of existence, it really was a fun time. Gigs were always excitingly on the edge of collapse into chaos. We played too loud, drank too much, and rehearsed too little. Still, it was never boring. I remember an occasion with bass player Danny swearing quite angrily that someone had stolen his pint of beer while he was playing onstage. When, actually he'd put it down on the (borrowed) bass amp and the vibrations mid-song had caused the glass to topple over, spill its contents down the back of the amp, and roll away. A fact that was only discovered when the same bass amp blew up midway through the set of the band we had borrowed it from!

Another time a drunken Richard (guitarist) decided to sleep in the back of the hired transit van rather than on the floor of the friends' house we were staying in after a gig in Leeds. Only to have a frantic girlfriend of one of the bands wake us up in the middle of the night shouting for the van keys. She'd looked out of the window as she heard Richard had made a lunge for the van window to throw up out of and dislodged the hand-brake, so the van was trundling backwards down the road unmanned with Richard still hanging out of the window!

All the Coventry indie scene at this time went to the same indie club, called Silvers. Every week you came home with a demo tape in your pocket to listen to, or you would wake up remembering you'd just agreed to join someone else's band. Again. Silvers is still there, though not called Silvers and with no indie night. We've just started having reunion nights booked there through a Facebook group at the same venue, with the same DJ's, and with the same old horrible carpets your feet stick to!

It's kind of refreshing to see so many of us still, at an age where we should know better, grinning and dancing about like we were 17 again to the old tunes. Then, equally amusing the next day reading all the Facebook comments about colossal hangovers, sore knees and cricked necks!

After The Balloon Farm came Perfect, who later changed their name to Dolores Haze. For me, this was THE band that probably should have been signed to deal that I was involved in. Both The Balloon Farm and Dolores Haze were good friends with other Coventry band Adorable who DID get signed – and to our dream label Creation Records (who later of course discovered Oasis).

There was always a friendly rivalry between the bands. We did gigs together, borrowed gear off each other, and members of both bands lived in the same rented houses together. Of course, I'd be lying if I said I wasn't a tad envious when they got signed. I believed Dolores Haze were as good. But really, I wasn't too begrudging, as Adorable was indeed a really good band, I still like and play their records often today.

So, that was my 'proper' live band experience that lead me now to The Pristines. It's funny to think that The Pristines has been the longest lasting and best known of all my projects. It was always a side project running in parallel to the real bands. Even the name was a joke!

I'd always recorded songs on the 4-track as demos to play with The Balloon Farm, Dolores Haze, etc., or just as songs unsuitable for either band that I still liked enough to make a recording of. It was around this time I started to become aware of and read the fanzines of the day. I could write another whole article on the importance of fanzines in the late 80's and early 90's indie. How they gave a voice to so many bands that would never get a look in the written music press, and were a million miles away from the mainstream. It's fair to say that fanzines back then would have been the equivalent of MySpace and Facebook in recent times – a place where anyone could get their music heard and to discover the undiscoverable.

But, I digress. I tend to do that.

I was lent a fanzine compilation cassette; coincidentally by Robert from Adorable who was in The Balloon Farm in those days, as his 'other' band The Applicants were on the cassette (see, everyone had more than one band on the go!). When I played the tape I was surprised to hear so many bands' recordings were homemade, DIY 4-track ones, and not professional (expensive) studio recordings as I imagined. This DIY ethic opened the door to anyone and everyone, some songs even sounded like they were recorded on a tape recorder in the corner of the room!

When I played the tape I thought, you know what? One of my songs wouldn't sound too out of place on this. So when I made a copy of the cassette for a friend at Poly I cheekily included a song of my own midway through, having to make up a band name for the track listing I gave him. Hence, The Pristines were born. A name that was chosen as he'd just bought the first Sarah Records compilation album, and of course *Pristine Christine* by the Sea Urchins was one of the first singles on that label. It might even be Sarah 1 come to think of it? He of course guessed it was me after questioning, but also said it was one of his favorites on the tape.

Buoyed by this I cobbled together 10 of my favorite "outtakes" onto a cassette, and made a sleeve via the old typewriter track list, newspaper cutting, Pritt Stick cut and paste & photocopied method! And sent it out to fanzines as *Honestly* the first cassette album by The Pristines.

To my utter surprise they loved it. I did other tape albums. I was allowed onto fanzine compilation cassettes for real. And, ultimately it lead to me being contacted by the wonderful Sunday Records in USA to go into a studio and record a 7" single, a subsequent album later, and to the recordings that still follow to this day on various small labels.

PART III – THE DEATH OF 'INDIE'

Which leads me to the final part of my ever expanding, and what's turning out to be a novella.. The hijacking of the term "Indie" and mainstream vs. DIY label ethics.

When I think of "indie" and indie labels I think of all those DIY labels that started in back rooms and split profits 50-50 with the bands. No contracts & all handshakes.

Think Postcard Records in Scotland, Rough Trade in London, Sarah Records in Bristol, early Creation Records, early Factory stuff, etc.

You can't underestimate the importance of these labels in giving a voice to bands that would never even get a look from a major label, and allowing them license to put their unique ideas and ideals onto vinyl. Indie music for me used to mean music for outsiders made by outsiders. Not just the shy bedroom-loner stereotype, but people operating outside of and bored of the mainstream with unique visions and often-singular genius. It was the kind of music when you discovered a new band for the first time it felt like they were *your* band, and that nobody else you knew had heard of them or anything like them before. This leads me to my oft-current rant of today – the death of the term "indie".

Don't get me wrong, independent underground DIY music that we all love still flourishes and will always do so. The internet provides so much diversity we never had access to in my youth. But the word "indie" has been hijacked by the major labels and their publicists as a convenient way to portray and sell any band with a guitar in it.

No matter they are on a major label, with stylists, an army of PR, publicists and massive advertising and promotional budget. No matter they are a middle of the road, safe, stereotypical, formulaic dross makers. You know the bands I mean, I don't need to mention names, and you all have your own lists in your head don't you? You can compile them as a pub game some time.

It started I guess with Brit-Pop. Suddenly indie bands were getting in the charts, snapped up by majors, and with a host of copyists in their wake also signed up to majors. Suddenly Oasis were as big as U2. The moneymen at the majors suddenly saw a new cash cow. It angers me they have stolen our "indie". Stolen our scene, our world, our badge of honor! If this means "indie" now – I no longer want to be associated with it. I invent new genres for The Pristines like "Gazedelia" (shoegaze+psychedelia.) I remember back in the early 90s getting my haircut before a gig that night and the hairdresser asking me if I had the day off work. I told him I did as I had a gig tonight, and he asked – oh, what kind of music do you play?

When I said "indie", he looked at me confused and said, "What? Indian?". I had to explain, as he'd never heard of "indie", as it being "you know, kind of like The Smiths or the Jesus and Mary Chain" as the only two reference points people had heard of.

I kind of preferred things when it was that way. Didn't you?

Jon.E.Hardy is the leader of The Pristines, a cult indie lo-fi psychedelic shoegaze (gazedelia) band from Coventry, England. With The Pristines, Jon has released six full length albums, and other various forms of releases on over a dozen labels around the world.

Casual Music Fans vs. Passionate Music Fans
By Matt Beat.

There are two different kinds of music fans: Casual and Passionate.

Casual fans make up the majority of music fans. They usually follow trends, and hardly ever go out of their way to discover new bands. Most often, they find out about new music from commercial radio stations, television shows, or movie soundtracks.

When they are teenagers, social pressure often dictates what they listen to. For example, if most of their friends are listening to Green Day, then it's highly likely they are also listening to Green Day. They never go to live shows by themselves. Usually at least one friend would have to show interest in going to a show before they decide they want to go also. The typical casual fan's interest in music peaks when they are in high school and college. This is when they are downloading the most songs and going to the most shows.

Speaking of downloading, that is the primary way in which they acquire music. For them, buying vinyl records or even CDs is just unheard of. They couldn't care less that a WAV file sounds much better than an mp3 or that nothing quite sounds as pure as a recording on vinyl.

A casual fan never goes to a local band's show unless they know someone either in the band or a friend of the band. They generally assume that most local bands remain "local" because they just aren't good enough.

When a casual fan has a favorite song, they will listen to that song hundreds of times, yet still not become sick of it. In addition, if they hear a mediocre song hundreds of times, they will mostly likely grow to like it (as long as they can sing along to it), even if they first hated it.

When a casual fan gets older, they stop listening to music as much. They stop going to shows almost completely, except for the occasional arena show. They dump much of the music they listened to while they were younger, telling others that they've "outgrown" it. By the time they are in their thirties, they are listening to talk radio more than music on their way to work each day. Casual music fans are rarely musicians, but when they are, they usually give up playing instruments by this time.

Passionate music fans are the minority. Most are borderline obsessive compulsive when it comes to their personal collection. They can talk about music for hours at a time, often having conversations that seem pointless to casual fans. A casual fan wonders "who gives a crap?" when passionate fans argue who was more influential: The Pixies or Nirvana?

Passionate fans sometimes follow trends, but usually go out of their way to discover new music. They'd prefer that their favorite bands never get too big, for two main reasons: a) so they can go to their shows without crowds or expensive tickets b) so they can appear more hip or cool to others for liking such obscure (yet critically-acclaimed) music. They most often find out about new music from word of mouth, music magazines, and, most importantly, the internet. Web sites like Pitchfork and the Hype Machine are integral in finding out about the latest, greatest stuff before their friends do.

When they are teenagers, passionate fans most likely begin in the "casual fan" category, but then break out in reaction to societal pressure. When they find their niche, they cling to it like family and often become very narrow-minded with their tastes. For example, fans of death metal in high school generally share disdain for country.

This generally changes in college, however, as passionate fans begin to branch out to many genres of music, finding the universal appeal of qualities such as melody, harmony, and complex rhythm structures. A passionate fan generally doesn't care if they are the only one in their group of friends that likes a certain band or artist. They'll even go to live shows by themselves.

The passionate fan's interest in music peaks usually in their twenties, but even after they settle down and start a family their interest never declines much. They never stop acquiring music, and often end up with a ridiculously large collection of CDs, vinyl records, and even obsolete formats like cassettes and 8-track tapes.

If a passionate fan likes a band, they will tell the whole world about it (as if the whole world really cared). They go to countless local shows, often treating local bands like rock stars before hype takes over. Because most passionate fans are musicians themselves, they empathize with other musicians trying to make a living doing what they love, while simultaneously envying other musicians when they achieve any sort of success that exceeds their own.

Most passionate fans eventually become disillusioned about mainstream music due to its appearance as a product, something meant to be consumed for profit without any regard for artistic integrity. Because of this, they are often called music snobs or elitists. By the time they are in their thirties, they are annoying casual fans due to their "childish obsessions."

While there are many differences between casual fans and passionate fans, most of us come to like music a certain way. We are not born into this world with Godspeed You! Black Emperor blaring on our headphones. Our environment mostly controls our destiny, beginning with our parents. I think the natural inclination for kids is to rebel against their parents. Therefore, if your parents listened to New Order, it is simply not cool for you to listen to New Order. Instead, maybe some AC/DC or Black Flag will do.

Another obvious influence is friends. Never underestimate the power of peer pressure, especially during the tween stage, when kids often will stick their tongues in toasters if all their friends are doing it. The tween stage is critical- this is often when kids begin to find their own identity separate from their parents and/or siblings (although older siblings usually do tend to remain influential throughout the teenage years). Disney knows this. They have capitalized on it well.

Nearly all of us are introduced to music through mass media. Most kids aren't going to check out Daytrotter or a college radio station on their own. There's a transitional stage to get to that point because the more experimental the music is, the harder it is to get into it. Before I liked Sonic Youth, I had to like Weezer, and before I liked Weezer, I had to like Hootie and the Blowfish.

By the time we are in high school, we think we've got it all figured out. Both casual and passionate fans completely disregard entire genres, simplifying kinds of music into neat categories. Going to live shows is mostly a social activity for teens. Songs are downloaded mostly on impulse. It is also during this stage when passionate fans and casual fans begin to materialize into two distinct groups. Sometimes, one may not become a passionate fan until much later in life, but usually by the time one is in their twenties, they are on a direct track and usually don't even think about getting off that track.

Matt Beat is a music junkie. With around 21,000 songs on his iPod, he's sometimes overwhelmed by how much great music is out there, most of it in the underground. He also plays keyboard, guitars, trumpet, and sings in the band Electric Needle Room, and is currently in the process of recording songs about all of the Presidents of the United States of America. He'll even break out the guitar occasionally while teaching high school social studies in Overland Park, Kansas. Along with his brother Steve, he also plans on filming a movie based on his adventures as a hospital valet manager.

How Can I Survive (When There Is No Money for My Bills)?

By Ola. Nyberg

Music always came first for me when I was younger, and even if I'm pretty old and have a family now, it is still important. Most of the music I listen to has been what you can call indie.

When I was young in the late 70s and early 80s, I began my journey into the world of music; punk and new wave were there for me to discover. Most of those bands were on big labels. I guess because no one knew how to start their own, but that changed.

There used to be a debate about making money in indie music. Some bands were called sell-outs if they sold a lot of records and made some money out of it. The hardcore indie kids dropped the bands and sold their records to the second-hand stores, even if the music was still good.

Then they moved on to the next cool underground indie band. Bigger record companies tried to buy small labels who had the new and interesting bands. Some sold their labels and became rich; some didn't. I have a friend who has one of the most legendary labels in Sweden. He was offered more than enough money to last him a lifetime and he would still be in charge of the label for the next 5 years. He refused. I was proud of him when he did it, but now I think it was probably the most stupid thing I ever heard. He barely survives now a days and he can't afford to make records with some of the bands who have been on the label from the start.

I guess I wonder: why shouldn't smaller labels and bands be able to make a living out of music?

I don't think anyone who is in the indie music business has the intentions of becoming multimillionaires, but they should at least be able to pay their own bills and be able to put out more great music for the listeners. I don't think that people who have a genuine interest in music can disagree with that. When you say that an artist has to suffer to be able to make their art, does that mean that they shouldn't be able to eat and pay their bills? They suffer when they go out on tours; playing for a small audience at a shitty club for gas money and crappy food, dreaming of a good hotel room and a bigger tour bus.

Here in Sweden when a foreign band plays at the clubs my friends run, they always get good food and most of the time they get a hotel room instead of an airbed on a hardwood floor at the club owners apartment. I know some bands actually prefer that, so they can cook their own food and have a more homey feeling.

When it comes to keeping it indie and still be able to make a profit, there is one label that stands out for me; Merge Records. It is a role model for how things should be done. Merge always kept it small and low key and they took good care of their artists. They made sure that the bands felt at home and shared their profits with the bands. I guess that's why most of them choose to stay with them. They have always been my favorite label out there and have almost always been on point when it comes to releasing new great bands. They have released some of my favorite bands like Superchunk, Butterglory, Neutral Milk hotel, and The Magnetic fields. In my opinion, some of the best indie bands out there. They have also re-released the first three Dinosaur Jr albums. That is an act of cultural goodwill right there if you ask me. With bands like The Arcade Fire on their roster, they make all the money they deserve for the many years of hard work. In addition, they have always been generous when it comes to freebies and they have a mail order service that is awesome, even to a faraway place like Sweden.

I do spend a great amount of time looking for new bands on the internet, and I download a lot of the music I have, but I would rather have a physical copy of the stuff I like. It´s easier for me to know what record I want to listen to if I can see it, than it is when it's on my media player. I have a love/hate relationship with that thing.

It´s easy to start your own label these days. The hard thing is to get people to buy your records. It seems like people want all of their music on their computers now, instead of on a LP or a CD. I think that's a sad thing. I personally can´t imagine my home without my records, magazines and books. It would be a pretty sterile and boring place to hung out in, and my home is where I spend most of my time. I really hope that people get back into buying records again, and that record stores can get back in business. There is nothing better than a good record store. I can spend a lot of time and a lot of money there if they are good.

The new wave of indie labels is going in a different direction, thanks to the internet. There are tons of so called CD-R labels that have discovered bands through sites like MySpace; and I love it. Great new bands are now given the chance to come out and play. These new labels are putting out compilations with great new bands for us to discover. I have been included on a few of them with my musical project, Before I Got Convenient. I sincerely hope that people out there buy the records from them. Even though it's a cheap way of releasing bands, I think it´s a good and new way of thinking. When you make those limited edition CD-R´s, the only thing that kind of sucks is the job of burning all the copies yourself. As well as making the covers. Usually, the companies don´t have a proper webpage where you can download the music. They can´t make too many copies of the CDs and they usually can´t give more than one free copy to the bands so it can be hard to find the music. I have done it myself through my own (now defunct) label, Ruskstate Records.

When my friend and I had Ruskstate Records, we gave half of the copy´s to the band for them to sell and kept the rest for us to sell to internet stores and from our MySpace page. So don´t forget the artists that make the music; they deserve their share of the cake. And the chance to pay their bills.

Ola Nyberg *is a musician from Västervik Sweden. He has been involved with the record labels Rhythmace recordings (which is still in business with bands like Burek V, Hellon, Korea Campfire, Eve & the Last Waltz, My way and Mats Grönmark) and the now defunct CD-R label Ruskstate records (with bands like The Mare, My darling YOU! And Little red Corvette). He Dj´s on occasion, and he is Swearing at Motorists favorite DJ. He and his friend have plans to open a cafe that hopefully will sell records and have live shows. In the photography field, He shot the cover for Kramies's EP, The European, and is hoping to do some more covers for other bands.*

Copyright
By Alan Cohen

copyright, copyright
you can't make music without making a fight
the author's not the owner's and those minds are closed tight
copy-wrong copy-wrong
you can't put poetry in a song
there's no more poetry to go along

copy-left copy-left
soon there won't be no copies left
if art appreciation's intellectual theft

copy-down copy-down
you can listen to the words but don't share them around
i can die today and sue you into the ground

copy-up copy-up
when art becomes a business and you start filling your cup
it's the soul you snuff
it's the soul you snuff...

Our War: A Race With Bon Jovi, Linkin Park & Neon Trees
by Elsa Faith

Why independent musicians are competitive

While Paris and Beijing were vying to host the 2008 Summer Olympics, the rivalry between the French and Chinese began to heat up in March 2001 when the People's Daily (the Chinese Communist party mouthpiece) declared of Paris that "certain urban areas leave something to be desired when it comes to cleanliness. In particular, errant dogs and rabid dogs are increasingly numerous." Claude Bebear, the head of the Paris Olympic bid committee, had a handy rejoinder: "Dogs are dogs," he declared. "They do the same thing everywhere... It's just that there are no dogs in China – because they eat them."

Competition – The basic human nature needs to compete. Just like animals, having dominance hierarchy is very important for us to develop psychologically. This aggression (not to be confused with violence) is not to be taken negatively as we can use it as a source of motivation.

In sports, athletes are well trained and know who or which team they are up against. Unfortunately, most independent musicians are unaware of their competitors. Naturally, if you are an unsigned act, you will feel that other unsigned acts are your competitors. Especially if you participate in 'Battle of the Bands' or 'Online Voting Contests' from corporate companies like Guitar Center, Converse, Musician's Friend, just to name a few. Media of course exhilarates this aggression and "gives hope" to us with "Reality TV" competitions like American Idol, X Factor & America's Got Talent.

Even though these competitions began with the idea to find "the best band/act" – now it is more a battle of popularity. Rarely these days, especially locally organized ones that we come across competitions with real judging categories such as 'Songwriting', 'Audience Interaction', 'Quality of Performance' and 'Originality'. Sadly, most times these competitions created a false exposure for bands and can encourage "cheat votes".

Along the way, most independent musicians forgot the reason that we chose to be independent. Most of us actually don't want to be signed to a major label. Even for those who want to, the big NO comes knocking on our door from those big A&R guys. We are not "good enough" according to the mainstream industry's standards. In fact, there's absolutely no guarantee that an act will be a success even after signing to a Major Label (remember Glam Rock to Grunge days, anyone?).

However, who should we compete against?

Who Gave Love The Bad Name?: Understanding Our Real Competitors

In the video game 'Left 4 Dead (L4D)', it is made clear of whom our friends (the other survivors) and enemies are (the zombies). If along the way, your friends needed life aid, you will help them. Their survival is yours too. It is a very simple concept if you are aware of the goal of the game and focused too. Also, if you play with an experienced player, you will be led to the right direction so that you won't get killed by sneaky zombies.

Every one of us has shared this experience. Your band practice diligently in the cold garage or attic and got enough originals for at least three full-length albums. Just like in the game, as a band, you have a goal and you're focused to achieve it.

Guess what? Many independent musicians from around the globe are just like you. They want their music to be heard. They check their Myspace play-list, friend request other bands and their fans and possibly write a blog – daily too. Just like in 'L4D', they share the same vision. They are not the zombies. Why? Because they are survivors and they face rejections just like you too. Who are the zombies then? Major labels are the zombies. They have major control of what bands have to sound/look like. Might as well eat our brains, right? Obviously, the zombies have the upper hand in this industry. They have products and their products are our competitors. Their products are the bands that we see on the charts.

Now, don't get me wrong. Like I mentioned earlier, competition is a good thing to feed our natural instinct. We should actually learn from our competitors and how their labels market them. Study these bands. If you're asked, who's on top of the Billboard Rock Chart this week, do you know the answer?

In 'L4D' there are several zombie characters that have unique behaviors. There are special ways to kill them. Review the Billboard Chart in your genre and study the bands. Notice their songwriting technique, their attitudes, etc. Study them before you "make the kill". Do you also notice the cross genre collaboration between a lot of artistes these days? For example, B.o.B featuring Hayley Williams (Paramore) and Black Eyed Peas featuring Papa Roach.

Have you ever thought of collaborating with other independent acts? You can collaborate in songwriting, performing, recording and even work with local artists to help you design your album artwork! This win-win situation has endless opportunities!

Yes, we as independent musicians can play the game like the big boys. Other than studying your competitor, treat competitions not as a battlefield, but a marketing playground. Use the opportunity to network with other bands, their fans and judges too. The Rolling Stones didn't become Rock 'n Roll legends just rolling around on their beds 24/7!

One Step Closer: Our Direction In The Future

The best thing about this race, is that there is no need to be number one. Depending on your band's goal, you might only need

0.01% of this six billion world population. There's room for success for everyone.

Plus, unlike the days before Internet, independent artistes can now promote their music while they're at home. It's unnecessary for musicians to leave CD consignments in record shops. We can even jam with other musicians from the other side of the world – LIVE! Since it's on the Internet, it's pointless to keep these findings to yourself (Google! I love you!). Finding all the support you can get and sharing information with others, you might actually stumble upon more gold!

Although Internet is convenient, leg work is still important. Here, in Portland, OR, we have support from our local community media. Do you have one in your area? If you do, give suggestions, if they don't already have a special on local music. How about volunteering your services?

There are so many possibilities for independent musicians to succeed if we put our heads together and not just depend on getting signed to a major label. Always look back on your goal and help one another.

Bon Jovi, Linkin Park & Neon Trees were once like all of us. At least we now know that we are all in the same race and running towards the yellow line together. Ready? Get Set! Go!

Elsa Faith flew to the USA from Singapore to meet the man she 'met' on Myspace so that she could audition for his band, Soul Distraction. She has been performing on stage since the age of six. Certified in marketing from Chartered Institute of Marketing (UK), she is always intrigued by clever ideas and loves to jump into positive world changing projects. At the 16th Billboard World Song Contest, one of her songs received an Honorable Mention.

Bucket Lists Are Bullshit
By Jess Gulbranson

Let me repeat myself: bucket lists are bullshit. Recently, my little brother's best friend died suddenly and unexpectedly at the tender age of 14. As a bit of grieving my brother decided to clandestinely form a bucket list and carry it out. You can imagine what would be on the bucket list of a 14-year-old boy. Regardless, the whole idea, which seems to be a relatively modern marketing spin on the ageless "things to do before you die" concept, is pretty vulgar. Sure, fine for people who know they're dying and want to blow some money, but what about the rest of us, and the rest of our lives?

In accordance with the statement above, I have no bucket list. I decided not to have one even before I knew such a thing existed, and I'd like to briefly tell you why, so I can segue into the important part of my message. Back in my early twenties, I was in a very strange instrumental jazz fusion-noir band. How's that for a pretentious concept. We managed to score a gig at a very large corporate picnic at a resort in rural Washington, which was like some magical fantasy land. Not only did we get to rock out on a big stage in front of lots and lots of people, and get paid to do it, but... get ready for it... the water fountains RAN WITH PINK LEMONADE. That is fucking rock and roll. So, fuck the pyramids. Even now I have trouble articulating what that experience meant to me.

One thing I realized years later, once I'd processed it, was that I had learned the value of just doing things and not waiting. If I hadn't decided I wanted to play music, and put the time in in the garage, I wouldn't have ended up on that stage. This applies in most other areas as well. I've wanted to be a writer since I was a little boy, and in little fits and spurts I have tried to do so. I really had trouble believing- understanding, even- that it was a serious undertaking that I could actually do. In high school I had some great teachers who encourage me and supported me (Victoria Wheeler, I'm looking at you), but through no fault of their own other than an ignorance that is global, they missed out on a crucial bit of info that I have finally figured out.

Cut a couple years forward. I am newly married to a crazy woman, and I have been roundly booted from a band just before a European tour. In a crappy ancient house in North Portland, I decide that I am going to be a writer, and build myself a little writing nook in a haunted stairwell. The internet was still in its toddler years, but I am brand new to it and suddenly I discover that there are places out there who want my writing. My successes are very few, my rejections many, but the important part is that I am getting myself out there. The level of quality I am putting out is still at the level it was in high school, which is important. If I had known that it was as simple as just writing something and mailing it off, I could have started years before, and gotten the awkward part out of the way!

Here we discover a couple of pitfalls. Not only did no one tell me I *could* write if I wanted to, but I spent almost a decade in an abusive marriage with someone telling me I *couldn't* write. Or play music, or act, or paint, or any of the ways I express myself. You may find yourself in a similar, though less extreme situation. Do not listen to these people. Listen to me, right now.

No matter how bad you are at what you love to do, or how untrained, or unmotivated, YOU CAN DO IT. Just start.

Opportunities will follow from there. Mind you, I am not trying to feed you some Law of Attraction bullshit. I am a Buddhist, so I am trying to feed you some of Newton's Laws of Motion, also known as *karma*, in its actual meaning. Whenever you do something- or refuse to do something- it has effects both on yourself and on the world. Maybe immediately, maybe later, but it is important to realize that you are not in a vacuum.

We're at a sticking place now. I have shared my own revelation about the limitless possibilities that exist, but understanding that these opportunities exist is not enough. You have to believe that they are there for you, and not just for some vague category of 'real' artists. So how do you start? The first way is to just start. If you play guitar and want to go further, play your guitar. If you want to write, then write. Our current level of technology is such that you don't have to write a whole novel on little yellow legal pads, or scrawl guitar tablature on a napkin. There's nothing wrong with these things, but since you're probably already at a keyboard anyway, why not write that story? Recording technology as well- it's easily within the means of anyone to start making demo-worthy songs at home without any significant outlay of cash. It might require a little help from someone more knowledgeable to get you there, but that brings me to the second way to get started.

Work with someone. Now, this can be finding a mentor type- guitar teachers are the most common form of mentor in this case. Or, you can start working with a peer. This may be inviting a friend or two over to play music casually, or it could be joining a band. You gain the benefits of other people's experience, and often it provides some form of creative accountability. A further way to work with other people is to join a group. Writer's groups are the most obvious form here, and the musical equivalent would be the open mic. It also may be as simple as finding yourself in a community dedicated to whatever art you're pursuing. I would not be a published author right now without the local 'Bizarro literature' scene and the help and opportunities they provided. That brings me to the third and final way to get started.

When you see an opening, take it. Now, I won't recommend that you skip the rigor of practicing your art, but sometimes it happens. If you are starting out fresh and new, and really can't get past that blank page, then find a submission deadline and go for it. This method helps, not only because it gives you a goal to shoot for, but it also may be the blow that kicks you over into actually believing that you can do what you do. Now, at this point you may be experiencing some version of *But I can't...* Ignore this. When the music blog I write for was notified by a major artist's PR people that their artist was open to interviews, I said "Sure, why not." Then

I found myself interviewing a 10-time Grammy nominee. Before I started, I of course felt that interviewing rock stars was only something that 'real' writers or journalists did. Spurred on by that, I found myself interviewing a founding member of one of my favorite bands since I was a kid, then one of the most legendary producers of all time, and so on.

I don't share these things to inflate myself. My achievements are actually humble, but figuring out that it was possible to achieve them was life-changing. There are plenty of people out there who are insanely talented- you are probably one of them. All you need to do is know that you can do it. Please, please, please listen- you can do it. It is never to late to start- and more importantly, never to early.

Can you taste the pink lemonade yet?

Jess Gulbranson *is the author of 10 A BOOT STOMPING 20 A HUMAN FACE 30 GOTO 10, MEL, and Antipaladin Blues. His poetry has been featured in Umbrella Journal, the Portland Fiction Project, and Bradley Sands Is A Dick. Also a critic, artist, interviewer, and actor, Jess makes music under the name Coeur Machant. He lives in Portland, Oregon with his wife and daughter.*

What Michael Larsen Taught Me About Art
By Alexander Hallett

In 2001, I was a pimply-faced 15-year-old high school sophomore with braces big enough to attract lightning, a gap between my front teeth that a semi could fit through, and arms about as big as a KFC mutated baby chicken drumstick. I think it goes without saying that I was quite the ladies man. Somehow, in the midst of all my social obligations, I rediscovered my love for hip hop via the then relatively new "underground" scene. I raised myself on the likes of 2pac, Wu, De La, and Naughty by Nature, but got disenchanted by the subsequent stream of imitators the record labels put out to make a quick buck (see: Sisqo). But then, all in one day, I heard Eyedea, Sage, Aesop, Atmosphere, El-P…it was like I was hearing my once cherished style all anew. Here were guys that were making music because they *had* to, not because they had to.

And, for my money, that's what makes independent music so vital to the continued progress of the musical landscape. That compulsion. That drive. That fire under your ass that makes you spend 14 hours a day in front of blank sheets of paper, weeks of picking at a guitar, and years of endlessly fine-tuning your voice, vision, and message. That need to take the skeletons out of your closet and make 'em pretty. Just because you *have* to. 99.99% of all of us musicians start out indie, some of us stay that way until we die, others keep the indie mindset even when signing to the majors, and others end up doing what they need just to make a few dollars and some fame. I'll probably be the first, and I hope I have the testicles to avoid the latter. The one person I knew who stayed truest to his artistic self was Micheal Larsen, who many know as Eyedea. In August and September of 2010, I was beyond fortunate and blessed when I got to go on the road with him (as well as Kristoff Krane, Cas One, and Sadistik) and shoot the shit with him for hours on end in my very own tour van. I never told him, but the guy was as close as it comes to me for a musical and artistic idol. Aside from

74

being fearlessly open to channeling any form of expression that came his way, he shrugged off the six figure offers after his Blaze Battle and Scribble Jam victories. And here I was, sitting in my van roaring across the country, absorbing every piece of knowledge I could from this man to whom the word "talented" doesn't nearly do enough justice. For my money, he will always remain the definition of why independence in art is so important: it allows the truest pursuit, realization, and expression of self possible. And he genuinely conveyed himself better than anyone I've known and reckon am likely to ever meet.

It is people like Mike that helped draw me to my path of personal truth through music. I started out recording in an empty coat closet, with an old video camera with the lens cap on to capture my vocals, a Discman with headphones playing the beat, and video editing software to edit the audio. I'd lock myself in the closet for 6-8 hours a day and record horrible take after horrible take after hilariously awful take until my voice was shot, and then I'd sit in front of my computer for another 4 hours to mix down one far from passable song. This start wasn't really the most logical approach to take to start making music, but it was really all that I had at my disposal. And, even though I'm still a ways away from fully locking in on my voice and artistic self, these sessions with my video camera are what started me on that path. You know, that whole journey of a thousand miles starting with a single step.

One of the most difficult parts of being independent, at least for me, is not allowing myself to get too caught up in stressing about "making it." Becoming envious of seeing some of my peers get larger fan bases, reach a broader audience, tour alongside some of my heroes. That's probably the biggest drawback that sometimes leads me to question what the hell I'm really doing all of this for? It's just important to recognize that for what it is, though: a knee-jerk reaction by my ego that wants what I see them get. And the thing is, I'm incredibly happy for my friends and fellow artists that break in. It's just fuel for the fire to keep the shoulder to the wheel and keep on going. Granted, it's pretty tough to make music if there isn't money to put food in my mouth, and it's ten times as difficult to continue to the pursuit of what I love if the well-being of people close to me is at stake. But I mean, hey…there are worse things than having a 9 to 5 to pay the bills if it means I get to do what I love 5 to 9. It really is the journey where the beauty lies.

And on that journey, we can lift each other up, one by one on each other's shoulders, to touch god with artistic heights we may have thought previously impossible, or we can – as I've done in the past – let the ego get caught in the game of "me vs. Them" and bring one another down so the art suffers and no one advances as far as they could. I think everyone has a great story to tell the world, and it's equally important to help others bring their story out as it is to tell yours for yourself. Mikey was a beacon that told his story while recognizing the value in everyone else's. And to do anything less than my best to continue the work he believed in would be a disservice to his memory and the influence he had on me.

Michael "Eyedea" Larsen died of an accidental drug overdose during the creation of this book in October 2010. He was 28 years old.

Alexander Hallett *is an independent hip hop artist, who makes music under the names Alexipharmic and Bodi. He is also the CEO of Elephant Memories, a socially responsible record label that donates 50% of its proceeds to various charities and global relief organizations around the world.*

A Tribute To Rudy
By John Siwicki

Ian Curtis gave his last live performance on May 2nd 1980 and that gig featured Joy Divison's first and only performance of "Ceremony" a song that would later be recorded and used as New Order's first single. A little more than two weeks later Ian Curtis was found dead in his home.

Rudolph Eberstadt IV, age 20, hung himself on September 8th, 2004. He played the drums for the band Shattered Society and later BEIA. He was a true lover of music and we even had a fake band together. We were called "Join The Imaginary Club."

It had been some time since I had seen Rudy and we talked about meeting up again sometime that month. I had been in England for most of the summer and I had just got back and started adjusting to life. I was working on that Wednesday evening when my sister called in a panic. I knew something was terribly wrong and that 3 minute drive home felt like hours and I nearly hit 4 cars on the way home. I rushed into the house and saw my sister in tears. She managed to get out a few words to me all I could hear was "Rudy is Dead."

I froze and just stared. I didn't know what to do. I didn't believe it at first. How could this be I thought? We are only 20 and death is not in our thought process yet. Life has just started for all of us, it has not ended. A few friends and I went up to Rudy's house to pay our respects to his parents and little brother. We stayed for a bit, sharing stories and talking about the good times. But, I wasn't really emotional. I wanted to feel more. I should have felt more. My dear friend is dead. I just felt nothing inside. I felt guilty about my lack of emotions. I wanted to cry but I couldn't. My mind was running wild of so many things and seeing everyone and his parents was just overwhelming.

I want home early that night because was supposed to go to class the next morning. It was the first week and I talked myself into thinking some basic math class would make this all go away. I couldn't sleep and I just sat there awake. Thinking and wondering the question anyone who knew Rudy would ask. Why? Why did this happen? Could I have done something? Did I miss a sign? Rudy would of given you the shirt off his back so it was hard to ever see those signs. He always was pumped up and ready to go.

My mind needed a record. Music was the only comfort to me most days. Everyone has awkward stories of middle and high school years. The moody and emotional British scene is what got my heart. I had recently done some record shopping so I had a few great items on the top of the pile. I went for New Order's Substance. I had been searching for the original versions of "Temptation" and "Confusion" on vinyl. This was going to the treat to get me to sleep to get me to do anything. I put the middle down on the record and the opening chords of "Ceremony" rushed through my headphones and knocked me over. My emotional wall was down. I felt something for the first time all day. I felt pain and I felt empty. Rudy is dead and I will never be the same again. I stood there in the middle of room with my hands in my face just crying. I must of played that song 20 times that night.

There was something comforting in the song. You can hear the pain and the emotion in the lyrics and the one of the song. It must have been a hard song for them to record because it was Ian's, and that it was awesome. I learned the back story later but it is a great example of the band paying tribute to their fallen friend. This is my tribute to Rudy.

John Siwicki *is the founder of Comfortcomes.com from Shelton, Connecticut. Since 2004, he has been covering the hottest stuff in the indie world. He works in marketing full time and one day hopes to harness his talents to make a movie. And one day release records under the name The Imaginary Club.*

Independent Music as a Signal
by Matt Montgomery

When the Arcade Fire were handed a Best Album Grammy, they didn't just strike a blow for indie music — a cultural shift was signaled with sweeping implications for popular culture and modern society. The win is admittedly a big one for the band, and it's remarkably easy for fans to praise the band's success as something it's not.

The Suburbs isn't solving world hunger. The world's ills aren't being confronted by the band — and they're even among the more socially active advocate-bands, what with their work following the aftermath of the Haitian earthquake. No, they are but one band, and they simply can't be the savior of the world. Still, their win is significant in one very real way: It's yet another road sign on the long trek toward a culture of independence in music, culture, and society.

It's important to recognize that the shift is not on the cards because independent music is receiving accolades from very mainstream circles — in no way is it a proximate cause of the change. It is, however, an effect of the impending decentralization of culture: It happens — and will continue — because the options for independent thought and artistic creation is becoming more prominent. It's a function of technology; it's a function of the power of people to create without being spoon-fed their tastes, perceptions, and ideas.

It's the 2011 Egyptian and Tunisian freedom riots, the 1960s Civil Rights and women's suffrage movements, the French and American revolutions. It's innovation: the first microprocessor, the camera, the light bulb, the alphabet. It is people being able to unleash their artistic outputs on a broad base without leaving their living room, and it is people spreading cries for freedom across Twitter and Facebook. It's people — the rational human at work, taking that which makes us unique and changing lives and cultures and societies and the world. It's people rejecting culture from on high, forming a society apart from the doldrums of the 9-to-5 and the ubiquity of bureaucracy.

Effects of the move toward independent culture cannot be overestimated. Gone are the days of endless Beatlemania and Lisztomania. Obsession will continue, but the fragmentation of popular culture necessitates that it can never happen in the same way.

When information, media, culture is not spoon-fed, people think. And they don't just think a little — they think a lot, and they think constantly. If not because they have to, then because they can.

The rumblings are underfoot, and popular culture will never recover from the shaking. It's the shaking that pushed the coalescing of the online piracy underground with the above-ground nature of music and created Napster — and it's the shaking that led to the privacy-concerned Tor network that has been vital in securing the freedoms of many around the world.

But the future is big, and the future is scary, and the future is uncertain. The ease of sitting back and letting culture come into view is gone. The multitude of cultural choices mean decisions must be made quickly, lest it all pass by.

The orchestra? The pictures? The opera? The indie rock venue down the road? Never mind, it's passed now. Without constant attention and vigilance, boredom is the name of the game. Solving it may be easy enough, but it's not entirely clear how, and it's not entirely clear it will be solved productively. The dangers are vast. The rumblings of cultural change signify impending fissures, and it's all too easy to fall between change and progress and end up somewhere in a deep rift, entirely unawares.

But the now-inevitable shifts are illustrious and inviting. They're for the people, by the people; it's the advancement of humanity by humanity. It's pushing forward when it's easier to stand still. It's living in fast-food culture and cooking dinner.

It's genre-agnostic: It's not indie rock, it's not hip-hop, it's not world music — it's progress without aesthetic preference. The decentralization of media has been heralded as the decentralization of power. It's not hard to see why. When perceptions don't come shaped in the official view, they have to be hand-crafted.

It's beautiful, staggering progress. The Internet culture of the 90s and '00s is being replaced with something more agile, and we're already seeing change. Independent music may have been the winner when the Arcade Fire's Win Butler stepped to the Grammy podium, but humanity was the winner when Egypt's Mubarak stepped down from power.

Matthew Montgomery is a music journalist who writes for several publications and founded an independent music-focused publication, MusicGeek.org, in 2005. He's been writing about music for 8 years after starting a rogue student newspaper at his high school, which ruffled a few feathers at the best of times. Unsurprisingly, he is now studying journalism and will be graduating from Southern Utah University in 2011.

Hold Tight London
By Anna Lynne Williams

I spent the first eight years of my life as a musician playing coffee houses and fairs, selling tickets to play shows, hand-cutting homemade artwork for cassette releases, recording vocals in an unlit closet. But about seven years ago things started to peak for me as an artist, when my band Trespassers William was promoted by Nic Harcourt on KCRW and we were nominated for some songwriting awards in Orange County. Around this point we received an email from Simon Raymonde of the Cocteau Twins, interested in releasing a single for us or possibly rereleasing our second album... and a few months later we were on a plane to England for our first international tour, booked to play dates with Explosions in the Sky, Azure Ray, Leaves, and Damien Rice. And to meet Simon. And to play on all of the big London radio stations. All of which had me so overwhelmed that I was curiously relieved that there was a ridiculous amount of turbulence on the flight overseas.

Most stunning of all had been a phone call from Simon a few weeks prior, asking if I knew who the Chemical Brothers were, that they had heard one of our songs on a mixtape and wanted me to sing on their upcoming record. I of course had heard of them and wanted to take a stab at it. They sent me a finished instrumental track and over the next few weeks I obsessed over coming up with lyrical and melodic ideas for it. I left the CD in my car stereo and sang over it on my way to work each day, calling myself on the phone and recording my ideas. Not knowing what they would be into, I ended up writing three completely separate songs for their chord progression. Everything fell into place, as the Chemical Brothers were going to be working in a London studio at the same time that I was going to be on tour there, and a date was arranged for me to meet up with them and sing, still not sure which of my versions they preferred or if the song was definitely going on their

82

album. I was 24 years old and intimidated. For as long as I was writing parts in my car, I was seeing the song as a puzzle that I was trying to complete. But at some point I was going to be shaking hands and performing, which is nothing like doing a puzzle.

I believe it was Valentine's Day, half way through the tour, and a black car was sent for me mid-morning. My manager came with me and gave me a pep talk and held my hand in the car. The tour and all of the radio interviews had been going well, but this was a final vocal for a Chemical Brothers album and unlike any other challenge I'd had, and I was still sleepy and my hair was still wet. I remember feeling jealous that my band mates had the day off. When we arrived, Tom and Ed were both there, casual and smiling and English. Their faces were familiar from magazines and they were very sweet. The studio was much more elaborate than any I'd been in (as I'd expected), the vocal mic was set up in a huge white room. They offered me a plate of cookies and my manager asked if there was any beer (which had proven useful at a few radio performances). Ed went off to a shop around the corner and returned with Guinness, which I sipped before singing to temper how surreal everything was feeling. There were other engineers and producers in the room, but I can't remember how many. It turned out they hadn't received all of the files I'd sent with my ideas on them (only the first one), so I was to sing all three. They set me up in the middle of the white room. When I checked the mic I already sounded expensive and reverby. I asked them to mute the drums so I could sing the vocals a bit more mellow.

I was in a little whirlwind and sang the three songs straight through to the loop. No punch ins or pauses. Tom asked me to sing the words "don't worry, nothing can go wrong" to one of the melodies I had come up with. To lighten up the song. Then they played back a few sections to have me try some harmonies. All of this must have taken about 20 minutes, then they said "straight out of the box" and I was back in the control room. They didn't play my vocals back to me and I really had no idea how it had come out. We started to talk about Manchester because Trespassers had a show there the following night, and it's where they had grown up. They recommended some bars and restaurants. Then I was back in the black car.

This singular experience of singing in such a high pressure situation so early in the morning in front of celebrities has never been equaled in the last seven years. I've since learned how to record myself and have my own gear, so practically all of my vocals are recorded at home, at my own pace, usually alone. Even when I collaborate on someone else's album, I don't enter their studios and look behind the curtain. I email them files.

It was months later that I found out which of my three songs they had chosen, that it was to be called "Hold Tight London", that it would be the fourth track on the record. The next January, right around the same time that I moved to Seattle, *Push the Button* came out and I received a few copies in the mail. A year or so later the album won a Grammy and their label sent me a gold record. Having had this experience at a young age didn't really break me in or change my expectations for the future. I have continued to feel a bit out of place at press conferences, or disbelieving if my band sells out a show in a city I've never been to before. I think it's a healthy part of being a public performer that sometimes you play to a room that is full and other times to just a few people who are talking over you. And for every glowing review there is an insulting one. And so my life is full of big victories and big wounds. But that session in the Chemical Brothers' studio will always be the first, the most intimidating, and the most widely listened to thing that I've participated in. I wish that I had been a bit more prepared and professional about it, but then I wouldn't have sung it the same way.

With a similar philosophy, I rarely edit my lyrics or sing things more than once anymore. There is always something about the first take, straight out of the box, that will never be paralleled. And this leaves me more time to write the next thing or record the next instrument, and move forward.

Anna-Lynne Williams *splits her time singing in Trespassers William and Ormonde, as well as her solo project Lotte Kestner. She also works as a music journalist, and has recently started her own label. Saint-Loup Records will have its first release spring 2011.*

Music Is Independence
By Kayla Mitchell

Music breaks the chains that tie us down.
we are no longer bound to the clicks and clique's humanity has created;
we are independent, we are free.

Music frees the soul; everything we've done or ever will do in our path to glory is merely a whisper in a world so full of man kinds righteous uproar.

Our hearts are forever compelled by the music we hear in our everyday lives.
When we are lost for words; desperate for an answer,
Music speaks.

We as individuals are free,
we are independent,
Just everyday people with the will to succeed.

Humanity may be so lost in war and greed.
But we as individuals have our music;
music with the power to set us free.
Independence is mankind's music.

My Back Pages
By Ryan Feigh

I have lived in Portland, Oregon for ten years and plan to be here for many more. But like most young transplants I spent my formative years in a place where the culture of creativity wasn't ingrained into the DNA of the city as it is here in Portland. In fact, some might argue whether my hometown of St. Cloud, Minnesota should even be called a city at all. I would argue that it should, and qualify that statement with the fact that it is currently the 3rd largest metropolitan area in the state of Minnesota behind Minneapolis-St. Paul and Duluth-Superior. That said, it is the kind of city that is very common in the Midwest of this country, one that takes pride in the abundance of national chain stores and restaurants that mushroom out from the main mall into every conceivable direction. It is a region where fine dining options are best exemplified by an evening at the Olive Garden, Red Lobster, or The Radisson Hotel. The kind of place where musicians that perform cover songs have a distinct advantage over those that perform original material in the few local bars that are fortunate enough to be equipped with some sort of stage area and/or PA system. While there certainly are exceptions, for better or worse, the fact remains that the prominent culture skews towards the conservative and the corporate in almost every aspect of the region's cultural identity.

The upside is that those who actively reject these cultural norms tend to find each other quite easily. Those who attend the rare underground show or volunteer to DJ at the local college radio station or frequent the independent record store are often able to connect on a deeper level than in a city oversaturated with such types. Or at least that was my experience in the mid-to-late 1990's. I turned 16 in April of 1992, at a time when the national media had begun to turn its attention to packaging Pacific Northwest bands as "grunge" and helped create and promote the idea of an "alternative nation". Were I a Portland native I might've been attending all-ages Pond and Hazel shows and rolling my eyes at Pearl Jam articles and dismissing them as ex-metal dudes from Seattle and a surfer singer from California who were cashing in our scene.

Instead I was a culturally isolated teenager who soon became convinced that bands like Smashing Pumpkins, Nirvana, Nine Inch Nails, and Jane's Addiction were downright revolutionary, specifically coinciding with my coming of age. Especially considering that just a year or two earlier I had been rocking out to the Top 40 hits of Paula Abdul, Poison, Tesla, MC Hammer, and Bell Biv Devoe. Although I now look back on that time with a level of slight embarrassment, I'm also quite glad that my ignorance allowed me to actively participate in what seemed like the monoculture at large being taken over by the new tastes of my peers and those slightly older than me. Which, due to the fragmentation of the music industry as a result of the present day information onslaught, will quite possibly will never happen again.

It should be obvious to most, but I can't help but stress the following enough. This was a pre-internet era, at least in my corner of the world. At the time our home computer was an Apple IIe, now a hilariously fossilized relic that could do little more than word processing, spread sheets, and only the most rudimentary of games. Even the simplest version of Solitaire or Chess was too high-tech for it to handle. So without the internet, SPIN magazine and MTV were truly at the cutting edge of musical information available to me at the time. My conversion to this new era of fashion and music was admittedly arrested and behind the underground it bubbled up from. I didn't buy Nine Inch Nails self-titled debut until a kid two years older than me informed me it was Axl Rose's favorite band for example. But though my adaptive speed may have been slow, my dedication soon became so fervent and all-encompassing that it was almost all I thought about for the next 15 years.

My senior year of high school I decided on a whim to write a music column for the school newspaper. I was already heavily involved in Theater, Choir, and Yearbook - activities that took a minimum of an hour or two of my time each weekday, often more. So I didn't think much of my music column, as I only had to spend an hour or so on a column every month and it came quite effortlessly to me. Being an adolescent obsessed with the first thought is best thought ethos of Jack Kerouac, I hammered out my music columns on a whim, a task that was much more enticing than finishing my Calculus homework. Considering that I now make a modest living with freelance music writing, this is quite amusing to me. In part because the activity I put the least amount of time and effort and hard work into during high school eventually became my true calling and also because as much as I love writing, it has become anything but effortless. While it has become the most rewarding activity in my life, it is also by far the most difficult. It is easier for me to work a month of soul-crushing food service work than it is to start a 150 word show preview. But if I finish that preview in a way I'm satisfied with, it's worth more to me than 5 years of food service work.

In the spring of my senior year of high school I applied for a job at the Electric Fetus, a record store that remains in business in downtown St. Cloud to this day. I enclosed a paper-clipped copy of my Top 5 albums of the year column, in hopes that this would give me an edge over other applicants. I actually ended up getting a call-back interview, although not knowing much about how real-world employment worked, I also mentioned that I would be leaving St. Cloud to attend the University of Wisconsin-Madison in the fall. At the time I was crushed that I didn't get the job, as it would have been an ideal way to save some money for tuition and spending money for my first year of school. In retrospect, I now realize it wouldn't have sense to hire me, considering I only would have been able to work there for a few months before leaving town. It wouldn't be long before I was back in St. Cloud though.

While I did relatively well grade-wise at my first year of college, it ended up being hands down the most difficult year of my life. I spent that year homesick, naive enough to be depressed at my inability to maintain a long-distance relationship with my girlfriend still back home in her senior year of high school, and disillusioned with the level of education I was receiving and the social life I encountered. Where I had imagined classrooms of highly charged intellectual discourse about the philosophies of freedom, artistic expression, or at the very least an outlet to express my ever-growing alienation, I was met instead with freshman lecture classes so large that I felt ignored and swallowed up by the system. My youthful dreams of weekends filled with unending intellectual discourse about music and art and its reflection upon our place in the zeitgeist of our time were met instead with gatherings in tiny dorm rooms filled with illicitly procured cases of Busch Light where the conversation rarely elevated beyond discussing the plot of that evenings Knight Rider episode we had watched on cable, or the still pertinent but soon played-out preaching to the choir argument that if we can die for our country we shouldn't have to go through so much damn trouble procuring these cases of Busch Light.

Had I not dropped out after my first year I have no doubt things would've had improved. But I was at a time in my life where I was the worst combination of precocious and naive. I wanted to have intellectual discussions about "the true meaning of the universe man!", but I didn't even know how to survive the universe contained within surviving freshman year of college relatively unscathed. I felt so utterly disconnected with my surroundings that I inevitably dropped out at the end of the year and returned back in St. Cloud dejected but determined to do something meaningful with my life. It wasn't easy to drop out, in fact being the oldest child of three, I knew it was my parent's worst nightmare come true. In a way it would have been much easier to stick it out to not cause my family any grief. At the same time I felt that I was destined for much greater things. The most difficult part was that I didn't know what that really entailed, I only knew what I wanted to reject, not what I wanted to embrace. Only time would tell.

I returned home and quickly found a job at Kinko's and a super cheap apartment with a friend of a friend. Being summer in a college town, my share of the rent was the obscenely low amount of $125/month which would then go up to $150/month once school started in the fall. I was hired at Kinko's with the promise of being able to work the overnight 11pm-7am shift once I learned the ropes from working in the afternoon. While I was able to hook up local bands with free fliers as well as cassette and 7 inch inserts, by fall it soon became clear I wasn't going to be promoted to the graveyard shift anytime soon. So I quit and started doing evening deliveries for a sub shop that closed at 2am which was much more conducive to my nocturnal nature.

I also started playing in a band with two other friends, Earl and Noah, which we dubbed Fa-Fa Fony which somehow made sense to us since Noah also played drums in the band Baba Booey. It was a band in the loosest sense of the term, considering we only had two cheap keyboards we would mess around on in Noah's parent's basement. For most songs we would use a demo or rhythm track for the entire song and then take turns screaming or rapping over the cheesy beats a la Wesley Willis. We never even got around to booking a show, yet due to a connect from an ex-coworker at Kinko's, we booked a couple of hours at a local studio to record. I'm sure the engineer had never seen or heard anyone like us before. Despite the fact none of us were yet 21, we arrived stoned out of our gourds with a 24 pack of Budweiser in tow, plugged our keyboards straight into the board and proceeded to tear through almost 20 songs. Due to my youthful exuberance at what seemed like an awesome opportunity for the band, I had neglected to let my work know I wouldn't be in that night, so the next day I found myself unemployed. Earl had a job as a line cook at a local 24 hour Perkins restaurant, and offered to put in a good word for me for a dishwasher position. His only stipulation for doing so was that I would not view the job as expendable as I had my last, as he was going out of his way to help me out. I soon interviewed for the position and was hired. My first shift was scheduled for Saturday evening to learn the ropes, and then follow it up for a brutal Sunday breakfast/brunch shift to see if I could handle it.

Then, seemingly out of nowhere, I got a telephone call from the Electric Fetus a few days prior asking if I was still interested in working there. I most certainly was, so I went through the interview process one more time, and by Saturday afternoon I got word that I was officially hired. I knew Earl would be upset at me, but this was opportunity I had been waiting for. Working at the coolest record store in town and having an all access pass into a world I wanted so desperately to belong.

The next couple of years working at the Electric Fetus were among the greatest of my life. The pay wasn't that great, particularly considering how much of my paycheck I spent on discounted CDs and records, but I was in my early twenties with very few expenses coupled with dirt cheap rent. Despite being hired in large part due to my hip-hop expertise, I quickly immersed myself in the entire canon of post-modern music. While I continued to stay well-versed in the genre of hip-hop, my co-workers turned me onto everything from Nick Drake to old Bob Dylan records to Spacemen 3. I soon took pride in my ability to steer customers towards the Wu-Tang solo record that might resonate with them the most as well as being able to expound on the Beck oeuvre or the local punk scene. I also was drawn to the history of proto-punk bands like the New York Dolls, MC5, and The Seeds which led me to a crash course in the MN rock history of The Replacements, Husker Du, and the Suicide Commandos. Dash it with Luna, a little pinch of Elliott Smith, and bake with Tricky sprinkles on top. I actively looked forward to work, couldn't wait to clock in and learn from my co-workers and spread my ever growing knowledge to customers.

But I was also kind of just a big fish in a small pond, just going to parties, shows, and trips to catch shows in the Twin Cities. Then, a few months after turning 21, I made a disastrous attempt to reenter college life at a local private school called St. John's University located about 15 miles outside of St. Cloud. I made this decision, in part because I knew I didn't want to be stuck in my hometown for the rest of my life, but also because I didn't want to stop working at a place that meant so much to me. I had also swallowed my pride and moved into my parent's basement at that time, and I thought that living in a dorm a short commute away while taking college classes would be the responsible grown-up thing to do. While those instincts were probably correct in theory, it ended up even more disastrous in practice than my first attempt at higher learning had been. This time around I didn't even last the year. Didn't even last the semester. Didn't even last more than a few weeks. Shortly after dropping out I was arrested for a DWI coming home from a party. My parents were heartbroken. I soon awoke to my mother sobbing and aching alone at the kitchen table pleading to God out loud. In her raw emotional state she claimed that due to the decisions I had made she felt like there had been a death in the family. I felt terrible. It was time for a change.

At that point what I really wanted to do was move to Portland, Oregon. I had friends who had moved there, who on return trips home for Christmas, convinced me that I belonged there. I looked into transferring to a school out there, but ended up settling on Hamline University in St. Paul, MN instead. I figured that it since it was a smaller school it would grant me the individual attention and discipline to not slip through the cracks as I had in Madison and without the God and football vibe that had permeated my time at St. John's. It was also far enough away that I could meet some new friends and make some new connections but close enough to make the transition easier on me and my family.

So I buckled down and spent the next 3 years doing almost nothing other than going to class, playing guitar and keyboards and messing around on my 4-track cassette recorder in my apartment, and going to shows at a bar called the Turf Club just blocks away from where I lived. Other than some Cultural Anthropology classes and a creative writing course, I learned far more at the Turf Club than I did at school. In my last semester I learned that Hamline refused to transfer my science credit from UW-Madison, so my only option to graduate officially was to take a summer Chemistry course in order to get my diploma. I couldn't wait as I already had my sights set on moving to Portland as soon as the school year was over. My friend Earl had moved there shortly after I got the job at The Electric Fetus, and was living in a house with his girlfriend which included an extra room empty waiting for me. The day after I moved out of my apartment in St. Paul I loaded up the bare essentials of what I owned into my parent's Suburban and drove with my mother riding shotgun straight across the country to Portland. I've been here ever since.

A lot has happened to me in the ten years that have elapsed since then. Shortly after moving to Portland and becoming immersed in the local music scene, I started a record label to showcase my friends talents that weren't getting the respect I though they deserved. After a few months at Earl's place I moved into a house one block north of Hawthorne into a house on 37th & Madison. My neighbors across the street included three girls who had just graduated from Oberlin and had a band called The Roulettes. My next door neighbor, Kevin O'Connor, worked as a cook at the hippest club in town at the time called The Blackbird on NE Sandy. He also had a musical project with a friend named Lisa and they called themselves talkdemonic. Kevin's college friend Sam often ran the soundboard for the The Blackbird and had just gone through the dissolution of his band Dutch Flat and created a solo project named Modernstate in the wake of that experience.

Amazed by the sounds I was hearing from my talented friends and neighbors, I armed myself with credit cards and started the label Lucky Madison. Kevin's roommate Paul designed the website and did the the artwork for the CDs. Our friend Skyler who worked at the Subway on Hawthorne had a studio at his dad's house in Camas, WA and offered to record bands for free in order to get a career in studio work started. The motto I created for the label was, "Deconstructing the Art/Commerce Paradigm with Passion over Polish." Little did I know I would soon be undone by my own idealism.

Before long the label blew up and we had international distribution and a strong local presence. One of the highlights early on was taking a trip with my immediate family to New York City and finding every one of my label's releases available for sale at Tower Records in Times Square. Start spreading the news and all that. Since I never signed any bands to contracts, and to this day don't regret working that way, we sometimes got acts scooped up by bigger labels such as Arena Rock Recording Company and Kill Rock Stars. Which I loved. A lot of people thought I should've been pissed about that edge of label ownership, but I welcomed it. Why would you not want a friend to get a better opportunity? The band I played keyboards in, Dykeritz, soon worked our way up from the shittiest of gigs into playing at super nice well paying clubs and local music festivals, opening for national acts as diverse as Dan Deacon and Rouge Wave while making solid connections with local bands such as Starfucker and The Helio Sequence.

Eventually though, while my wildest dreams had come true, it was more than I could handle. The more successful the label got, the more it drove a wedge between my friends and myself. Power corrupts, and I soon found myself bickering with bands over licensing deals and feeling forced to only sign artists guaranteed to tour nationally over amazing underground acts who couldn't afford to do so. So there soon came a time where it just stopped being fun and exciting to me. Most of my friends and family marvel to this day how I came to turn my back on all that I had worked for, how after becoming so successful so quickly how I could just turn the entire operation over to Kevin for nothing and just walk away. The answer is simple. Due to my success I slowly started turning into everything I initially had despised and fought against. Be careful what you wish for. In my misguided attempt to deconstruct the art/commerce paradigm I ended up getting swallowed whole by the commerce monster that is inevitable within a capitalist system.

Make no mistake though, I have no regrets. The Roulettes are currently playing regular gigs in their new home of New York City. Skyler no longer works at Subway and now makes a living recording local bands. Kevin and Lisa continue to tour the country with talkdemonic, despite Lisa's brief stint as a member of the Decemberists. Paul makes a pretty good living doing websites and artwork for local businesses and bands.

More importantly, I've witnessed people like my friend Sam marry and have a beautiful baby boy and continue to make amazing music that will likely never make Pitchfork headlines or blow up the blogosphere. That's what impresses me the most. The ability to balance an artistic self-worth outside of what the mainstream considers a success. That said, I have no ill will whatsoever towards those that choose to play the industry game and succeed. I'm a realist, I've never accused anyone of selling out as if it was a negative thing and I never will. I actively ache for the artists that I love to get the opportunity to do so. Yet, more often than not, my personal champions never get there. But that still doesn't diminish their contribution to my life. So, ultimately I hope that those of you out there who are making music or starting a blog or doing improv comedy or painting or making videos or writing about what you are passionate about or planting a garden continue to do so because it fulfills something in you and spreads your true nature and spirit into the world in a way that can't be measured in dollars or cents. Personally, I've since moved on to writing about one of my first musical loves, hip-hop, for The Portland Mercury. And while the monetary rewards are damn near non-existent I still feel very blessed to have the opportunity to speak openly and honestly in a public forum about something that makes me happy and continually inspires and energizes me. Real talk.

Ryan Feigh is a journalist/novelist from St. Cloud, Minnesota, and currently resides in Portland, Oregon. He writes regularly for the Portland Mercury, where he shows endless support of a hip hop scene that regularly gets overlooked in the city of roses, as well as writing for several blogs and publication across the country including the cult favorite Crappy Indie Music The Blog!

Music Sweet Music
By Phil The Tremolo King

Does the creaking of an old door make a chord? And if so, is it major or minor? Is the hum of a chainsaw really a kind of avant garde industrial punk rock? And what composer will ever write a more beautiful song than the bird outside my window is singing?

I remember…another time, another place. The Dogz. Three suburban teenagers banging out primitive riffs in my grandmother's attic to the despair of her neighbors. Blood on the strings of my cheap plywood guitar. We were way ahead of our time, and the hippies who saw our one and only gig did not appreciate it.

But life was not good. The blue meanies and the black crows were after my soul, but I was smarter. I escaped to the wilderness of the Big Apple, and reveled in all its rotten beauty, its glorious decay. I painted the cave dwellers, Diogenes living in a cardboard box looking for a human being on the streets of Gotham. I banged on my six string, shooting from the hip in various musical combos, for assorted junkies, homeless and drunks in the dark dungeons of the East Village. My brothers and sisters in arms were lost souls just like me…their beautiful dreams and wild creations the only way to resist. To exist. If we were a family it was a dysfunctional one. Forbidden fruit took a cruel toll on these frail and brave souls. We were canaries in the coalmine, pointing out the shape of things to come. Not many wanted to see… Alas, we lost the battle but not the war. Our beautiful decaying streets with all their chaotic found object poetry became overrun with strange deodorized creatures with cell phone in one hand and Frappuccino in the other. So off to greener pastures…me, my newly found soul mate and her son.

Off to the Big Easy, to look for the ghosts of Jelly Roll Morton and Sydney Bechet roaming the streets of the French Quarter. Bent and slurred notes falling from magnolia trees like overripe fruit. The Mississippi gurgling a soft slow second line beat, its brown muddy water rippling in mad arabesques like the

97

ironwork on the balconies of the old French houses on Chartres Street. Everything here is done to a beat…eating, drinking, talking, driving, loving…dying. Death is all around me, children killing children over a pair of sneakers while the fat cats suck oysters in their uptown mansions.

Then a madwoman whose name starts with K blew all of us out of here and scattered us far and wide all over the map…Mother Nature's cruelty and man's stupidity conspired to kill one of the most amazing cities in the world. And almost succeeded. (The stupidity was mostly that of the Army Corps of Engineers, FEMA, and …. But I digress). We returned, older and wiser, and picked up the pieces of our lives. And so it goes.

Through it all music has been my friend, my guide, my guru, my passion, my addiction.

Once in New York I jammed with a guitarist who claimed he had played with Johnny Cash. He had a ponytail and a plaid shirt and a beat up Telecaster. He mostly nodded, or stared. But when we played together, there was a moment where our eyes met…sounds good, bro. A connection.

Music is a universal language. It transcends what divides us. I've played an open air festival in Belgium for 500 people, a squat in West-Berlin for a crowd of drunken punk rockers, a country bar in Alabama for an audience of rednecks, a diner in New Orleans. I've played the NYC subway and world famous CBGB's. I shared the stage with my friend Vic Ruggiero from legendary NYC ska band The Slackers. I backed up a Russian mime in a theater in New York's West Village with a Russian trumpet player, a Ukrainian clarinet player, a Japanese bass player and a talking drum player from Ghana. I even played stand up bass behind Delfeyo Marsalis and Dr. John one time.

I went indie before indie was a word. My first cassette *Songs from Planet B* was recorded on a four track with a little toy keyboard, an echo pedal, a guitar and a SM58. This was years before anyone coined the term "Casiocore". The bands I was in played in squats and at house shows. We didn't play top 40 or grunge. We didn't have a name for our style of music. We played what we felt on whatever instruments we could afford. We didn't have illusions about being cool enough to get a major label deal. Some bands I knew did catch the brass ring...for most it didn't work out well at all. It sounded more like hamsters running on a wheel...working for the man.

One of the most satisfying things for me has been to see the music industry turn around completely, or maybe I should say come full circle. DIY is cool. Lo-fi is cool . Doing your thing is cool. That's how the whole thing started and only when it got away from that did music begin to suck. I'm hoping major labels are well on their way to making themselves irrelevant. Because all over the world musicians are taking control of their careers and their lives. And that's how it should be.

Punk rock, or its offspring indie music, was always about playing by your own rules. Fuck bosses. Fuck corporations. Fuck hidden agendas. Fuck posers. Fuck using music to sell SUV's. And maybe, just maybe, we can show the world at large a thing or two about living life to the fullest, not just chasing dollars and keeping up with the Joneses.

Meanwhile, I mind my own business and continue to explore the thin line between order and chaos, beauty and ugliness, happy accident and just plain ol' God-awful noise. Here in Snoball Studios life is good. The soft glow of vacuum tubes and VU meters, the hiss and static of a pawnshop guitar amp, the 60 cycle hum of an old plastic Bontempi keyboard keep me company. Music continues to flow from my hand and mind, haphazardly immortalized in ones and zeros or just on a plain thin piece of brown magnetic tape. And once in a while, I luck out and hit on something that makes me go...damn...that sounds good. But never as beautiful as the song the bird outside my window is singing. ..Nope. Not even close.

Phil the Tremolo King *has been a squatter, house painter, mover, illustrator, book seller, hobo, and street musician. Born and raised in Belgium, he's lived in Brussels, Berlin, New York, Austin, and continuously lives in his own universe. He now resides in New Orleans with his wife. He loves Tom Waits, the Archies, John Cage and bossa nova. Holed away in his Snoball studios, he bangs, plucks, hits, and blows into various implements to create what he calls 'Trem-O-Phonic pop'. He sings into an old pair of headphones and mixes on a boombox. His newest CD "11" is available from Norman Records in the UK. He wishes you all a very nice day!*

About Us, Random Calculator
By Alessandro Paderno

It's 1988. I'm in my cousin's room. He introduced me to Pink Floyd just few months ago. He and his friends during that weekend recorded some funny songs with just one mic.

It's 2010. I'm 32. I will not be remembered as a "man with good memory", so I can't remember which songs my cousin recorded, but I know that for a few months I asked him to play that tape again and again. I loved the idea behind this tape, and all the noise, ambience, mistakes. I guess this is how I started to be into music not just from the "listener side" but from the "producer/musician side".

I've always recorded all my albums by myself or with other friends. I've built up two studios, starting from a room, a mic, a tape, and eventually ADAT and then digital recording.

Now I run a small studio with my friend Fabio, who is also the co-founder of my band, Le Man Avec Les Lunettes. That is a swell way to remember how the things started and what's been going on …

With my band I usually use the studio for practice and, of course for recording. We've recorded a lot of songs there, spending many hours doing so… but not solely. The idea behind the studio is to give a possibility to bands that I love to record in a kind of "professional way". A lot of friends of mine are musician and usually they cannot afford a professional studio so they record in their room with one cheap mic/garage band/etc … this could be good, but I believe that every musician's dream is being in a studio with good/old microphones with time to spend to find the good sound, their personal sound. In Random Calculator (this is the name of our studio) a musician can spend how much free time we (Fabio and I) have and they can use every organ, guitar, bass that in we have collected in the last 10 years. Being in the studio gives a band an opportunity to make new and special sounds. As you can image this is not our work, we don't make money from this.

Payments are always welcome but if someone pays for the trip to reach Italy to come and play in our studio we can't ask him/her/them for more money. I'm very unhappy with the way money is managed and distributed throughout the music world (also in the whole world but this is another big issue), and maybe this is a way to fight it!

How do we choose bands? Friends, bands that we like ... the only rule is to spend good time in the studio, no additional stress needed! We have had people from Italy (of course), Iceland, Sweden, Norway, Denmark, USA, etc ...

I like working on my own material, for my band, as well as for myself. But, I learn a lot from working on other people's music. One process informs the other. I never think of myself as a producer when I work with other bands I just help my friends with their mixes or recordings ...

Random Calculator is essentially an apartment. We record drums in the basement. The microphones are usually close to the washing machine (turned off ... of course!), salame, and clothes. Upstairs we have 4 rooms and one bathroom. The 4 rooms are really useful for live recordings, as well as the bathroom. Both for personal use and for reverb! We can't afford to use analogue tape, and we don't have too much free time so we prefer to use a computer. But, we're buying old mics and old instruments that always sound better than new ones. We also have a kitchen, which is the most important place in the studio. We have lovely "piadine" made by an American girl, a special Swedish midsummer dinner, etc ... Or when we are in hurry a really fast takeaway pizza.

So, recording an album is something that doesn't necessarily require money and moreover. In a "kind of" real studio you can do something new with the sound that's not just going to simply sound live ... it's great.

Alessandro Paderno *was born in a small city in northern Spain, 1978. He is a very busy man, he has a wife, and he is trying to be "one of those fathers who take much responsibility". He likes Phil Spector, old microphones and Rough Bunnies. He records music.*

Not A Real Band
By Dan Abbott

There's a pivotal bit in The Matrix in which Keanu Reeves's crappy portrayal of Neo first becomes aware that he's been living in a cybernetic dream world. "This… this isn't real?" Morpheus, the pied piper of meta-space meta-consciousness, answers with a maddening counter-question: "What is 'real'? How do you define 'real'?"

While this has no doubt led to untold hours of bong-hit philosophy, it is a serious question that everyone has to grapple with at some level or another, some sort of firm foundation upon which we ground our beliefs, our fears, and how we judge the world around us.

What are the hallmarks of reality? Is a Facebook friend really a friend? Is it a forest, or a fiber plantation? Can you ever really be alone while talking on a cellphone? And in the art world, is a toilet seat art? Are comic books considered literature? Is Bobby Joe Ebola and the Children MacNuggits a real band?

The last one is a question I've had to answer many times. My buddy Corbett Redford and I play in an acoustic duo called Bobby Joe Ebola and the Children MacNuggits. We started in 1995 on a whim, and just kept on writing songs and playing shows, partly because we both needed a creative outlet that didn't require ammunition, and partly because it was so much fun. But as an acoustic band in a world of amplifiers and horn sections, we ran into plenty of musicians (and fans) who questioned the legitimacy of our form.

At that time in the East Bay, there were really only two places to perform if you were under 21 and in a band; 924 Gilman Street and the Berkeley Square. 924 Gilman was then just getting famous as the womb of seminal East Bay punk bands like Operation Ivy and Blatz. Out of the same amniotic fluids sprang the more listener-friendly pop-punk sound exemplified by Lookout! Records bands, and successfully mass-marketed by Rancid and Green Day.

The rest is history, as they say, but at the time, the east bay punk scene was going through a real epistemological crisis. What did it take to be a "real" punk, now that any suburban mallrat could buy spikes at Hot Topic and bands with two and three chords were all over MTV? What happens to outsider culture when all the outrageous anti-fashion signifiers become fashionable? The lines between genres hardened as "real" punks attempted to hold on to their identity. There was an explosion of "-cores" as the once diverse Gilman scene splintered. Once a haven for truly "alternative music", where not categorize able bands like Mr. Bungle, Moe!Kestra and Crash Worship had once played, Gilman now closed its doors to anything that did not wave the punk rock flag. Needless to say, an acoustic band from the suburbs that wrote funny songs about poop and politics was not even in the running.

Berkeley Square was less bound by ideology. Located on University Avenue in Berkeley until its closure around 1996, this bar served various kinds of "food", greasy technicalities which allowed them to put on all-ages shows. It was a slightly sleazy dive, where underage girls and cocaine both regularly disappeared backstage and were never heard from again. This was where Corbett and I each saw our first punk bands, and where our friends and their freaky bands would play. Our pal John (later our backup singer, and now known to the world as the vocalist for Fleshies, Triclops!, and Street Eaters) had a nerdy psychedelic funk band called Annulus which at one point was drawing in a respectable Friday night crowd, and frequently played with some of the aggressive funk-metal bands that were clogging clubs at that point. Our pal Thom Tucker was in one of these, a cartoonishly violent outfits called Impact, and we first played Berkeley Square when Impact kindly shared their set time with us. We went over pretty well, and were often brought on in between bands to do 5 minute sets. We were known, and we were liked, but that didn't mean we were respected.

Even when we were finally granted official stage time, the other bands tested microphones and openly tuned their instruments during our set. When confronted, they seemed completely surprised that we would object. "You guys aren't even a real band," we were told without irony (or, oddly, malice). We didn't have amplifiers. And it was just the two of us! And we were funny! Obviously we were not "real" musicians. If this had been a one-time occurrence we would have laughed it off. But it became a pretty common obstacle for us, not just at the Berkeley Square. Bands and audience alike made it clear to us, sometimes in the form of backhanded compliments, that what we were doing, and how we were doing it was not a band but a "novelty act".

Granted, we bore all the outward signs of a novelty act. Our first CD, the self-released "Two Cats" EP, had (to our giddy delight) been played on Dr. Demento's syndicated radio program, alongside some of the dorky musical comedy we'd loved as children; the great Tom Lehrer, The Toyes, and "Weird Al" Yankovic. We were clean-cut looking white suburbanites and we weren't even singing about chicks or beating people up. Some of our early songs were commentary on current political situations like the '96 presidential election. Songs that had a shelf life. In other words, novelty songs.

But so what? Are you really going to tell me that because Weird Al writes novelty songs, he isn't a real musician and songwriter? Have you *seen* him play? Let's see *you* do an accordion solo with one leg behind your head. Yes, he parodies pop culture and lampoons one-hit wonders. But he is the master of his craft, a superb musician and vocalist, and in my personal opinion does not get enough credit for his original compositions.

And in any case, lampooning contemporary culture is an ancient art form. In medieval times, troubadours were something like a cross between Weird Al and Fox News. Using recognizable standard melodies, these musicians (often in the pay of the rich and famous, but just as often itinerant wanderers) would craft new lyrics to comment on wars, plagues, weddings, taxes and the like. They would sing in taverns, where their wit could earn them anything from tips and free wine to a serious ass-kicking. This tradition survived in various forms, from the Star-Spangled Banner (adapted from an old British drinking song) to Punch and Judy routines.

So the fact that we wrote funny songs about, among other things, Bob Dole's moral crusade against pornography and violence, "Two Cats Running (The Ballad of Bob Dole)", gave some credence to the novelty act label. What irked us was that this gave people tacit permission to like us, but not respect us, as artists. The fact that we didn't have a rhythm section meant that, unlike other bands, we could not reach people in the same way. Our appeal was not in sweet-ass solos or beats that frotteurs could grind against strangers to. We were and are more of a cerebral act; we infect people not with grooves but ideas. But you know, Corbett and I had plenty of ideas in high school too. People with less ideas and more style got the respect and the chicks, and that's the way it goes sometimes.

But you know, we like to laugh. All the time. That's how we cope. And so yeah, a lot of our songs are funny. That doesn't mean we don't mean it. It's like the old S.P.A.M. Records motto: "Just because we're funny doesn't mean we're joking." Some of the subject matter of our songs deals with a very dark world, one that isn't going away with something as easily as revolution or apocalypse. I doubt too many folks would want to go to a show to see me and Corbett cry into our poetry books. And honestly, we would get bored with being sad and angry all the time. Sometimes the truth can be laughed at. Does laughter make the truth any less true, or less real?

While it's fun to see people standing around laughing and having their heads rebooted, sometimes it was also a little like being a handicapped boy watching the other kids play basketball. We knew we'd never have a mosh pit for an acoustic duo. And at times we even wondered to ourselves; *are we real*? Meanwhile, we released our own albums, ran our own record label, toured extensively, and put on free, illegal generator shows we called Geekfest. All the stuff a real band would do, only it was us. The punk rock community more or less ignored us for reasons of fashion. We took its lessons and applied them. We were never a punk band; I think it requires a little more flag-waving than we were willing to do.

I'd like to think that Corbett and I earned a modicum of respect through sheer tenacity, or even artistic merit, but maybe the times just caught up to us. The world of music has changed sufficiently that if our band had just formed today, we probably wouldn't have to deal with any novelty act stigma. For one, Dr. Demento is no longer on the radio. Acoustic comedy acts that have come along since we formed, like Tenacious D and Flight of the Conchords, have at least given people a frame of reference, even if it's a little irksome to be told we're like a band we predate by several years. But whatever. The recent folk-punk explosion, too, has neutered the "rhythm section want ad" argument, and there are plenty of acoustic soloists and unusual musical configurations that now get legitimate artistic respect that just wasn't there 15 years ago. I don't know that we played any role in that; we broke up in 2000 and were encased in carbonate for nearly a decade. But it's nice to see. And since the world has become so bizzaro-world effed-up that most people can only ingest their news through comedy, people might even start taking *us* seriously.

That was a joke, folks.

Dan Abbott *has been a journalist, anthropologist, carny, activist, musician, performance artist and food service drone, and has not entirely given up on any of these. One of the co-founders of the S.P.A.M. Records/Geekfest collective, he now lives in Oakland, Ca. He and plays guitar and sings with Bobby Joe Ebola & the Children MacNuggits, and Thee Hobo Gobbelins. In his spare time he plays D&D and invents new kinds of food.*

Independent Music and Community
By Cyndi Kimmel

For centuries music has served as a means of bringing existence together. Regardless of its roots, style or genre music allows things of nature & our individual and collective selves to be made realized. Though it affects each of us differently we comprehend music as a universal language used to express everything seen, thought, felt and done reminding us of our shared commonalities. Presently no genre of music instills such a feeling of community as pervasively as the independent music movement.

While we explore this idea it is important to first recognize what is intended by the term "Independent music". The phrase should not pertain so much to the trend of anything being "Indie" (Urban Outfitters, Twilight soundtracks, second-hand stores with raised prices because they know people are into thrift and vintage these days, etc.). Instead the phrase is an intended focus on the independence of music from major commercial record labels and boundaries. Every aspect of independent music, from the recording to the publishing to the performances, is more often than not created without direct involvement with or of the commercial Music Industry.

As the Western-world progresses music, reflecting our circumstance, changes. The shift within the past century from music being a primarily frivolous artistic endeavor to a respected profitable industry has encouraged the macro-focus of western music from the communal to the commercial. This coupled with the evolution of the listening experience from album to single has brought us to a swamp of quasi-talented musicians producing nothing more than hit singles. As a result the digital age is a detriment to the music industry, an effect that can be made positive if we work in remembering music should be art instead of commerce.

This is not to say Independent artists cannot or should not be financially successful in their pursuits. Though fiscal security as a result of their work is certainly something they hope for, it is usually not the primary motive for their making music. Instead success is achieved through their intentions being rooted in *music*, in the art of creating it, first and foremost. From this we receive a "feels like home" spirit of song; with familiarity in theme, simplicity in production, and intelligence in structure all blending together to create music ultimately more communal and accessible than most commercial music being made today. We find ourselves in music made incarnate.

The idea of music as something incarnate is nothing to be afraid of either. To describe our experience with music in such a way is simply to recognize song as capable of being made comprehensible. Our circumstance therefore, both as our own self and with each other, can be embodied by music. We create it, listen to and share it as an extension of ourselves. Luz Mendoza of Y La Bamba expressed this idea well during an interview I had with her about the creative process when she said: "[M]usic is your home, philosophy, sanctuary. We're playing music because we need it to keep ourselves in check."

Surely an unfathomable number of people pursue music (whether Independent or Commercial) for the reason Luz spoke of, as a means of keeping oneself balanced. However I have yet to see this balance pursued as purely and shared as freely as is done in the Independent music world. Yes money is nice and recognition is enjoyable. But to ground music solely in the achievement of fame or accomplishment is to miss the necessity of song. True music, music as it's meant to be created and shared, moves us to explore, question, and commune while remaining inhibited by commercial thought or agenda.

Music moves me. I feel it always; in everything seen, thought, and done. I am not alone in feeling this way. To create music is to offer a part of ourselves to the world around us. To listen to music is to accept, and therefore share, in the offering. As pioneers and lovers of Independent music I hope we continue to do just this. I hope we can remember, progress, and share this truth: As we sing, praise, live, destroy, die, scorn, heal, celebrate or morn; all facets of life, of each other and of conviviality can and should be held to song.

Cyndi Kimmel is a stage performer and writer currently living in Pullman, Washington. She finds a great thrill in discovering new music, and sharing it with the world. She splits her time with the theatre as a DJ at KZUU in Pullman at Washington State University where she has been acclaimed for showcasing some of the finest independent music in the world.

The Sergeant Sparrow Story
By Angel Russell & Spencer Thurlow

I was surprised when Angel asked me from the back seat of my old pickup if I wanted to be the Editor of her Magazine, Sergeant Sparrow. I had picked Angel and her boyfriend up hitchhiking and was giving them the usual post college spiel; yes, I graduated college, no, I don't have a job that pertains to what I'm doing, etc. In fact I didn't have any sort of job. It was the end of the summer and everything that was summer was falling apart and I didn't know what I was going to do for my first free fall in eighteen years. It was also the first time I'd gotten a positive response to the "I'm an English Major" thing. So I said yes, over the drone of the failing catalytic converter and her boyfriend's beard.

We decided to meet the next week. I was aware that there was no office space, no plaques on the wall and no shining paycheck at the end of the week, but I was positive. Our first meeting was held in a shack on a farm. There were peacocks and other animals, which would squawk and interrupt us, and the whole thing didn't last very long anyway because halfway through uploading, the computer crashed and died. It seemed like a failed venture, but Angel insisted that we meet the next week anyway and see what happens. This was the beginning of my experience in the indie music world.

We were dirt poor, and because of that some things moved very slowly. We couldn't just go out and buy a new computer. The computer wasn't the first setback that Angel faced. After coming up with the initial idea, Sergeant Sparrow Records and a solid mission statement, she sustained withering criticism from all quarters. In her own words; "The first time I got turned down was when I went to a business counseling office. I didn't have very much experience running my own venture so I turned to them for help. I had a mission statement, a website, and knew how I wanted to run things.

They told me in no uncertain terms that I didn't know what I was doing and the idea didn't sound that great. I knew that my idea was worth believing in. I went ahead with the issue anyway and sold out of my first printing! That's when I knew I wasn't going to give up on it."

It wasn't too hard to predict that perhaps the local business counseling office would condemn the whole thing, but the assault from elements of the arts community was worse because it felt like a betrayal. "The second time I was set back was when I found an office space in a small arts community. Next door to the office was a media arts company that filmed musician's shows and interviews along with a variety of other community events. Downstairs was a coffee shop/venue that hosted many nights of music. Across the way was an art gallery. I was sure that I had found the right place for Sergeant Sparrow and that together we could create a great artist community. But when I sat down with a couple of the owners, I discovered that the media arts company did not want me moving in. They told me that my business was in direct competition with theirs and if it was up to them they would never choose to have a record label/magazine next door. I was crushed. I didn't see how we were competition because I was in print and they were in film. It made it very difficult to discover that not only were business experts opposed to the project, but now people in the arts community were against it as well. For the second time I decided that I wasn't going to let them stop me and I found six more artists and released my second issue. I sold out again."

This was all on top of running the label, having a full time job, and going to school at the same time. But good things happen too. The reward of finding new and interesting music is almost worth it in and of itself. The more we worked on Sergeant Sparrow, the more people became aware and involved and the more I became interested as they kept providing input.

Since we're not a huge company we have the lightness and maneuverability that allows us to grab an opportunity when we see one, and also the trust and intuition that lies in making a decision quickly. Because we promote other Do It Yourselfer's they promote us and we all work together towards an end goal. We now have two editors, an intern, a comfortable base of contributors, and an ever-growing pot of friends for our meaty musical stew. Exposing original music that you care about is one of the main reasons the Indie music scene exists at all, and the network of reciprocity that results from this. The willingness and goodwill of the people who do support you makes the attacks worthwhile. For instance, despite the destruction of our computer at my first meeting with Angel, we cast around for a new one through all the channels we had and she was able to acquire a used computer free of charge from a friend. As a result, my duties as editor were not limited to a one week deal.

To date, Sergeant Sparrow Records has been running for a year and a half. There are eight albums, three issues of the magazine, and we continue to find and release new material. Angel will always keep it down to earth because that's where she started. "When I first started I sold my CD's out of a suitcase at music events and while on tour with my band. I handmade everything. I scraped by and persisted and now I have a lot to show for it. Don't let those who shut you down stop you. Find those who want to help and encourage you to keep going. Surround yourself with positivity and prevail."

Angel Russell *is the founder of Sergeant Sparrow Records and the Editor-in-Chief of Sergeant Sparrow magazine. Her intent is to provide people with new and exciting music through a serious of publications, releases, and a radio show on WVVY FM Martha's Vineyard.*

Spencer Thurlow *is an Editor of Sergeant Sparrow Magazine. He drives a busted pickup and his hair gets all messed up when he's editing. He is on constant watch for new literary works.*

Beat The Competition
By Jeanne Betak Cleemann

Courage.

I've followed the ways of CLEEMANN – a Copenhagen based DIY one-man-project. Writing and recording his own material independently, he is a man for whom art is life. His investigations in the tricky art of writing music is waiting for inspiration, holding a constant patience with a subtle material, starting the itch from scratch, over and over again. He does not ask for his art to pay the bills. He has patients to care for.

Unite.

Working independently is the most exclusive platform an artist can choose for. And only with extensive help from friends, fans and by the developing of a solid independent music society – imagine a combination of iTunes and WikiLeaks – it will become a realistic platform to work from.

Hope.

Independency is about words. Words performed by indie-labels, promoters, bloggers and twitters within the blogosphere. Free men and women, their words stood by friends and followers – young independent souls transmitting via word of mouth their personal musical gems within a bottomless digital ocean.

Love.

The People We Meet & Some of the "Now"
By Christopher B

The people we meet, is one of the most fascinating things of which many encounter in the world of music. Whether you be a music lover, a musician, or a promoter, it is realistic to say that you will almost never predict whom you will meet and what your experiences will be, which can lead any one of us to assume our encounters are often fortunate events which allow us to create a bond between others we may have not previously known personally, a bond which is created from a certain level of like mindedness , similar interests or perhaps a meeting as simple as an introduction of a new friend from an already known friend. Let there be no secret to these bonds which have been created, through which many of times are rewards received in exchange for the chances that we take and the hard work of which we do each and every day. Through and through, ultimately it is our undeniable will, is to not solely let others seek interest in our work, but it is also important to seek out interest of others in support of our work.

One of the most genuine ways to create a collaborative relationship is music is from the bottom, and to allow time for growth in collaboration and to provide for your best chance to continue the relationship in the future. Regardless of specific size of your project, whether it be small, medium or large, one thing is certain, we will always be working from a pool that has various occupancy rates. There will be times that the "pool" is overcrowded, and there will be times that the pool will have room for you and your friends. Very much like the world around us, the music community is ever changing, in recent years at rates likely more rapid than they've ever been before.

Due to ever change and overcrowding in certain areas of the music community, there is still space for each and every one of us of which wants to contribute to our own projects and or to support others' projects too. You're never going to know what the perfect timing is, often times you have to get yourself up off of the ground and have your humble beginnings regardless how the current times are or the opinions of others, as we know what is best for us, and we hold the right to decide what we think is right to do and as humans, we are able to adapt and adjust to situations as we see fit. Due to the ever changing music community in recent years, it is likely linked to a variety of assumed factors, and just because some of your favorite blogs, venues, bands, radio stations, record stores or record labels are calling it quits, doesn't mean it's time for you to do the same. When those situations occur, you should allow yourself to be even more open-minded and to embrace the resources out there of which still exist to support our endeavors.

Although these circumstances create frustration and missed connections, for the amount of time spent on water under the bridge, you could replace that time by investing more time into others, thus creating many more new leads and personal connections with others. As we all know, many music projects have a shelf life, of months or years, and in some incidences some projects last for a decade or more, but is important for our own projects survival is to not be distracted by the folds, and instead focus on new sights, as there is always connections waiting to be made, amongst people already out there and people soon coming, connections amongst many of which are near to us, but haven't quite been touched on as of yet. I am not like everyone in the music community, I consider each and every one of us as unique, and no better or more deserving than the next person regarding opportunities that are out there for the taking. I feel they all should be earned and offered on a fair basis rather than to be guided by politics and back door/under the table interests.

I must admit I have done many things that not many people can say they've done before, and I've also done some things that no one may ever be able to say they have done before, but the point is you do not have to be a copy cat to make a mark, there is an ever importance to doing your own thing, on your own terms, that's what makes you who you are, it is a part of our personality. I am ever proud to not be sequestered, and to have opened my doors and have worked with musicians from all around the world and with pride, dignity and great honor to each person I have worked with. I am ever grateful that through my bedroom label Series Two Records based in Columbus Nebraska USA, I have been able to work with bands from all over the USA, Canada, Mexico, Argentina, Peru, Costa Rica, Denmark, Sweden, Norway, United Kingdom, Taiwan, Japan, China, Australia, Indonesia, Thailand, Croatia, New Zealand, Latvia, Ireland, Germany, Belgium, Poland, Russia, France, Switzerland, Spain, Italy, Finland, Brazil, Singapore, and Israel. All my efforts have been purely selfless, and put forward with the intent to help others that are grateful and selfless too, of course not everyone we may meet has the best intentions, but we owe it to ourselves to give a chance to those whom present themselves with the best intentions for not only us, but for our friends and supporters as well.

I am involved in many selfless projects today in addition to Series Two Records, another project of which has my active involvement with the multinational Nebraska Pop Festival, a gathering of friends meeting new friends, people having fun and hearing fun new music. Nebraska Pop Festival has been a good excuse to meet some of the people I have already worked with from abroad, and to also meet many new musicians and fans. Nebraska Pop Festival is a testament to all the hard work that myself and others put forward, a gathering which has made hundreds of people proud each year to be a part of and to witness.

Christopher B *is the founder and sole operator of Series II Records and the creator/organizer of the Nebraska Pop Festival, an event featuring independent artist from all over the world, from Omaha to Copenhagen. He is active also active in developing compilations and other events to support a VRIO (Value-Rarity-Immutability-Organization) framework he feels that everyone should follow, all the while supporting the independent music community.*

Finding Satelite Jameson
By Antonio Navarro

My first encounters with music were in the late seventies, when I was five or six years old. My father ran their phonograph in my house's kitchen with many Sinatra, Fausto Papetti or Los Indios Tabajaras' songs. My mother would be singing beautiful Latin songs around the house like 'La Cucuaracha' or 'Mamy Panchita' while performing domestic tasks. I find it strange to think now that there was so much music in my home, but the school I attended was void of any. There was no subject of music at that time, and only the French teacher could be found singing songs that we were yearning to learn. However, music was all around out of school: radio, TV, the street market vendors sing gypsy tunes.

There were other things that would interest and guide me through adolescence into manhood (meccanos, football, sketching my classmates, studying, etc.). I was also used to regularly attending mass (which I still attend not only because I am a Christian, but because this is where I learned to play guitar). But it was music that transformed me in a sense. Perhaps simply by curiosity. I strongly believe that because music did not exist within my schooling, I gave it more attention. And of course there was the influence of my father who was a sculptor. I began to manipulate and change the chords of songs in my head. I began to hear the tunes emitted on the radio at the time, and I began to reconstruct them in different progression that I felt was in much greater style.

Some years after that, I gradually began to compose completely new music myself. I would compose pop music because it was what I heard constantly on the radio. And while on this medium, I must say that there was a very important moment in my life when my parents took the radio from its original place atop the refrigerator, where I could not reach it very well, and brought down to the kitchen table directly in my reach. In that moment I took control of the dial. I began sailing around the waves of the new music adventure. It was around 1988 and 1989 that my musical

119

tastes changed from the more pop-oriented mainstream (such as Level 42, who were the artists behind my first cassette purchase with their album *Running In The Family*) and found my taste moving towards so called "indie" groups such as Slowdive, My Bloody Valentine, and The Wedding Present.

So, around the late 80's my interest in music most definitely grew, which became very evident to my parents as I would sit during dinner with my new transistor radio stuck to my ear listening to Discogrande, a Spanish indie program that always featured the best of the local indie music explosion that was happening. But, my parent's didn't see these changes with positive eyes. Pop music in that era, especially in my own small city, seemed very dangerous. They feared that my future would be just another sad tale like Robert Smith (Disintegration was my favourite at the time). So, I switched gears, and chose to study Architecture at the university. To draw is my other great interest. In fact, to hear music while drawing is some kind of perfect to me.

But, music never left my mind. And recording my own music soon became a necessity. But it would still be ten years before I would arrange and compose music that would lead to building a career as an engineer. When money was available, I could reach independence. I would buy equipment and gear from indie labels and other second hand means. I began to record seriously in an old garage that had been converted into studio with two friends. Shortly after this kicked off, I joined a collective of people who ran a radio station in town. I participated in a musical program called El Buen Vigia (taken from a song title from the Spanish indie band Family). And throughout these advancements, I began to offer music that I had crafted myself through the radio waves and the internet. There were about seven years of uprising and terrific moments to happen.

After a bit of radio experience, I began to read as much about music as I could acquire. I also began to write about music through blogs like The Pop Page! (now defunct), Musica En La Mochila, and People Like Us. Around this time I discovered the powers of social networking, specifically Myspace. It was now possible to have my music become an influence to, as well as being influenced by, so many great bands around the world. It was no longer necessary to hide in the shadows. And I soon became in contact with some wonderful folks who helped me release my music to the world. I received support from the likes of Series Two Records and Aplasta Tus Gafas de Pasta who would edited some of my music to CD-R form, all in the name of independent music. I do not receive payment for the few copies my music might sell. For a payment taken from those who truly love independent music at such a large capacity, would simply take away from their efforts to run their labels, and to edit other emerging artists just as they once did for me. And, well, I simply enjoy being paid in recognition. That is how independent music should be ran, anyway.

The perfect song is like to doing a circle with the hand, and after many attempts, it comes almost perfect. It is like the perfect blue of a clear day; it is like an orange juice in the middle of the summer; like that film that you never want to finish. It's those special moments when your girl looks at you in silence with an accomplice smile. Sometimes it's like a tennis match that you started losing and you finally won. It's that song that have all the notes that it must have, no more and no less. That song that is related with that moment in your life you will never forget; while you hear or play the perfect song you feel a discharge from your nervous system epicenter to your legs, or you start to dance around with the rhythm or start to singing it in front the mirror or your friends. The perfect song takes you on a trip to another landscape or city and perhaps you can imagine the perfect video clip for it.

A perfect song is just like when someone that you don't know may say something that you are thinking in that exact moment. Sometimes this can be very difficult, like playing Minesweeper and completing the panel without any explosions (impossible!). Or when trying to finish a 1,000 piece puzzle. Even terrible songs can become perfect songs with a few chord changes. It's like a good magic trick. Only God can stay behind the perfect song because men and women are his perfect work, therefore you are the perfect song.

Antonio Navarro *is a 37 years old musician from Albacete (Spain). He began composing circa 1987 around thirteen years old, driven by the beautiful songs in the radio. His first recordings didn't materialize until 1994 as* **Satélite Jameson** *on tapes that never seemed to stop coming until recent days. One of them (which was recorded and arranged with friends Miguel Angel and Juan Carlos) was edited by a little Madrid-based label Aplasta Tus Gafas de Pasta in 2007. During the period of 2002-2009 he ran a radio program called* **El Buen Vigía** *about all kind of music and eras and was selected in 2003 by readers of Rockdelux press as one the best national musical programs that year. In his second life he is a building engineer.*

Cats, Coffee, and Recording Music
By Joe Holtaway

Your instruments and coffee cups are on the floor, lyrics around
your knees and evening pulls to night over your room.

The cats are running their races under the window in it all.

Hit the record button again – the tape turns and you sound your
words, take up the strings sing over yourself.

It's all whispers, chords, clicks, claps, verses and choruses rolled in
together and replayed through headphone wires from your loyal
machine across the floor and up into your ears; while the cats run do
their jumping under the window in it all – the colours of the
evening.

There's joy in the playing, there's joy in the sounds, joy in the
words and there's a 'collecting it all up in one place joy'.

Music is What Made Me
By Will Silvey Simons

I was in seventh grade—1996—when I first experienced live music that was unlike anything I'd heard on the radio or on television. On a late summer evening, my best friend and I were dropped off by one of his parents at Sokol Underground, a dank rock club in the basement of a social hall in a south Omaha neighborhood. We were there to catch some local rock bands at a show billed "Anti-EdgeFest." The "Anti" part came from the fact that a few miles away several chart-topping and MTV-friendly bands like the Verve Pipe and Semisonic were drawing thousands of people together for the biggest one-night stand outdoor festival in the area, named "EdgeFest," all put together and promoted by the now-defunct alternative radio station 101.9 The Edge.

But down at Sokol Underground, several local bands who were totally overlooked and unsupported by The Edge were preparing to hold their own little festival. Which was really nothing more than a five-band bill versus the typical three. My friend and I were the first two kids to arrive at the show, with only a bartender, a guy in his mid-20s, there to keep us company. He casually talked to us and apologized that the show was starting so late. It was slightly disheartening because, as 13-year-olds out on a school night, there's no way in hell our parents we were going to let us stay to the end, so we hoped to catch the first two or three bands before the scheduled arrival of my father at 8 p.m. to pick us up and deliver us home. To make peace, the bartender offered us some complimentary 7-Up to help pass the time. We obliged and drank it over ice, shot straight out of a sticky bar gun. It tasted rubbery, was flat and discolored due to being mixed with cola.

Eventually the first band arrived after an hour or so of us just sitting there with the bartender. The anticipation began to build. We were going to watch a rock show! How cool we were compared to our friends sitting in the grass and nodding their heads to sleepy one-hit wonder rockers–quite the contrast to our view of a tiny stage in an empty club. We moved from the bar to a table in the room for a better view. The band, called Revilo, was not what I expected. The guys in the band looked like older versions of my friend and me. Just normal, slacker dudes with ripped jeans and Converse shoes. They had scruffy facial hair and reeked of tobacco. They set up their amps and drums and tuned their guitars, and soon began mumbling poetic nothings into the microphone, resonating out through the PA and over our bodies.

Sadly, we were only able to catch about two-and-half songs before my father arrived. Regardless, it was that night when the idea of playing music in a band was no longer a pastime reserved only for the flamboyant assholes who moved to L.A. to make records for major labels. No, I realized anyone can pick up a guitar, learn some songs and book a show and people would come to support you, even if it's just two teenage kids trying to mold their own unique figures out of the clay soil their hometowns were built upon.

It is over a dozen years later and I'm in a van with five people I love more than words can describe. These people, one of them the very same friend I went to Anti-EdgeFest with years ago, have become extensions of myself. We make music together and operate as six-headed monster—a rock 'n' roll band. We travel across the US like a caravan of minstrels, performing our delicate pop music at dank and musty rock clubs in Toledo OH, Richmond VA, Madison WS, Lawrence KS, Denton TX, Jamestown NY, Des Moines IA, Bloomington IN, Chicago IL, New York City and elsewhere. We bicker with one another and laugh at the same stupid shit. We are ambassadors of Omaha, spreading the wonders of our beloved hometown across the nation. Back at home, the present day equivalent of EdgeFest is taking place (something called "River Riot," I believe). We weren't invited to play and we couldn't care less. We don't belong there. We belong on the floors of our friend's dirty townhouse in Columbus OH. We belong on the Staten Island ferry with our dear friend and makeshift tour guide Quinn. We belong in the basement of a house in New Brunswick NJ playing our songs for 20 sweaty Rutgers students. We belong on an empty stretch of beach just north of downtown Milwaukee, skipping rocks along Lake Michigan. And our friends are back home working their day jobs. Fuck some of us even have day jobs, too, but we aren't afraid to leave them behind for a few weeks in order to explore the many seedy music bars of America after dark. Yeah, we are experiencing the world in a way only the struggling musician can— through the eyes of Kerouac and the spirit of Sid Vicious. And we wouldn't change a thing if we could.

Will Silvey Simmons *decided in late 2010 that everything he does career-wise from now on must involve music or writing and hopefully both. He's currently an editor at Omahype.com, and the former managing editor of the Omaha City Weekly. He's played in bands since he was sixteen, most recently in a group called Thunder Power. He also helps with publicity for Slumber Party Records, a small independent label based out of Omaha, Nebraska, the city where Will happily resides with his instruments, records and two cats.*

The Wolf That Was Never Caressed
By Sanna Larsson

No one caresses the metal scene, claims Henrik Arvidsson in Swedish newspaper Dagens Nyheter. And truly no one does. However, the heavy metal scene won't let *itself* be caressed. At least not like a guinea pig in the arms of a reckless child whose parents are mainstream and commercialism. Rather, heavy metal is a loner wolf, only carefully scouting the borderline of mainstream society, occasionally showing off its rabid teeth in the midst of masses seemingly solely driven by moral panic and "what's on the radio?"

This wolf does like the occasional tickle under the chin, and its fur inevitably shines with more luster as soon as it gets to show its anti-mainstream sentiments. Or so we think. Because heavy metal fans aren't only world champions in loving in the dark, as states Henrik Arvidsson, they are also masters of the art of hating in the open, keeping all that is vaguely inauthentic and sell out while constantly stating its independence. Because what can actually be more important for a subculture which has survived four decades of scolding, parental advisory and which has, at times, been kept alive through a complex net of tape-trading contacts, than to think of itself as standing strong and vital? It's still aggressively protesting what is considered the wishy-washy "rest" of the music world. And what can be more important than collectively keeping this, however fabled and mystified, image of being outside and independent alive?

No doubt about it – defying the magic of the music to some – the heavy metal music in itself is in part riding the wave of commercialism. Swedish death metal band In Flames received the government "Export prize" of 2005 and as of the summer 2010, Swedish heavy metal festivals are popping up like mushroom after rain. Of course, these are only ripples on the surface of the heavy metal ocean, a testimony to the spread of the music. What is really at stake when talking about the heavy metal culture and the way it's guarded as a creation of independence by its fans is just that: the fans. Heavy metal is the love child of millions of diehard fans who refuse to give it up in favor of a late modern interchangeability. This child has come to being primarily through loyalty. This is what emerges when people need to stick together in order to uphold something of value. It is also what gives the heavy metal culture momentum against a world that is believed to never have let them exist in the first place. Last but not least, and sadly, loyalty is also what can develop into narrow-mindedness and chauvinism, which has been showcased on numerous occasions in heavy metal history.

I, however, recall a particular situation where the positive connotations of heavy metal loyalty and independence came to the fore: The sole founder, money bag and powerhouse of the small scale heavy metal festival "2000 decibel" was ridden with financial issues after a series of bad weather festival years (I was fortunate enough to visit the festival on an occasion where it merely poured, as opposed to hailed!). In fact, due to this, the founder was now on the verge of personal bankruptcy. Striving to cling to the remnants of his economic being, a few heavy metal journalists came up with a brilliant idea: He fought for us in a time where heavy metal festivals were scarce, now let us fight for him! The result was a mini festival (wittily named "200,000 Decibel", since that was the amount of money owed). Five of the most influential death- and black metal bands of Sweden at the time agreed to play for free, forsaking the chance of those much needed gage money. And the fans agreed to pay the excessively priced festival tickets, knowing that the money would end up in the pockets of Mr. 2000 Decibel. What I love about this scenario, though is that it indeed bears resemblance to any given episode of "Extreme Home Make-over" or similar charity-proned TV productions, is that all it took was that one person and his wish to bring metal to the fans in order for people to assemble around him. That mini festival felt sweeter than most and I´ll be damned if the musicians didn´t in fact go that extra mile on stage too. Or so we thought.

A co-worker of mine worried about her son being involved in the heavy metal culture because she thought of it as a hateful culture. And yes, as stated, hate is part of the equation, but it´s primarily directed towards not being able to stay in one´s own unique shape, not fitting in and hence to feel the need to take place in that parallel universe. The other part of the equation is helping a man on the brink of desperation. In essence, heavy metal fans probably spend more time loving in the dark than they do hating in the open. At least when it comes to everything that surrounds their music.

Ultimately, all people who indulge in independent music are in some sense loner wolfs, it´s the disentangling from the outside and the accountability and loyalty of the inside that are so important in instilling value into one´s own treasured music. It is the make-believe of a world of music that turns it into "true". As for me, I keep my wolf in the backyard, tickling it under the chin on occasion. I´ll even let it have a go at my mainstream neighbors once in a while to prove my heavy metal worth. Or so I think.

Sanna Larsson *is a PhD student in sociology at Örebro University, Sweden. She has been a heavy metal fan for 15 years, the last of which have been dedicated to interviewing and researching bands and private actors for her dissertation on heavy metal and identity construction.*

No Encore?
By Shawn Fogel

I voted for Ralph Nader in the 2000 Presidential election. It was the first time I was eligible to vote. I was sure he wouldn't win, but I felt comfortable voting with my conscience, especially because I was fairly confident that Al Gore *would* win. Technically I was right, but that's a whole other story.

I spent the first term of President George W. Bush as a student, at Hampshire College, a very small, very unique, and very liberal school in Amherst, MA. I grew angry and frustrated while I watched the President use the tragic events of September 11th, 2001 to foster a climate of fear, dismantle our personal protections and rights in the name of national security, and deceive us into an unjust invasion of a country that posed no real threat.

As the 2004 Presidential election began to approach, I felt there was much more at stake than there was a mere four years ago. The consequences of a second Bush term would be catastrophic, and voting my conscience took a backseat to voting Bush out of office. This was only my second Presidential election being of voting age, and I became engrossed in it. I had just graduated from Hampshire and was living in the next town over, Northampton, MA. Amy Goodman, host of Democracy Now, was the keynote speaker at my graduation ceremony, and I began to make her hour-long independent world news broadcast a part of my daily ritual. Air America Radio had just launched, and I would stream their progressive talk radio programming from my computer throughout the day, with The Al Franken Show being the highlight. That summer Franken released his book, *Lies and the Lying Liars Who Tell Them: A Fair and Balanced Look at the Right*, which I read several times before the election (intermittently roaring with laughter and clenching my jaw in anger). In the fall I canvassed for the DNC, going door to door trying to collect donations for John Kerry's campaign. It was difficult for me because I was rather lukewarm about Kerry. I strongly favored Dennis Kucinich during the Democratic primaries. Kerry was good, not great, but contrary to the core principles of voting in a democracy, I was more concerned with Bush losing than with Kerry winning.

I was devastated on election night when the corporate news channels began to call the election for Bush, but I regained hope when Vice Presidential candidate John Edwards took the stage and announced that the Kerry campaign would not give up, and would not stop fighting until every last vote was counted. I remembered how close the 2000 election was and I knew that it could be days before there was a clear winner. It could even end up before the Supreme Court again. I was far more devastated when John Kerry emerged the *very next day* and delivered his concession speech. I didn't vote my conscience *and* the candidate who I not only voted for but also did what I could to encourage others to vote for just conceded. It was a dark time for me, and a subsequently darker four years for our nation.

Third time's a charm, right? In 2008 I would vote in my third Presidential election, and this time it would be different. The George W. Bush presidency was over, whether he liked it or not, and someone new would be entering the oval office. I was now 26 years old. I had moved to Montclair, NJ and was living with my girlfriend. Older and wiser, I was ready to roll up my sleeves and do my part in making sure this election would move our country in a positive direction.

The news media focused on Illinois Senator Barack Obama and New York Senator and former first lady Hillary Clinton as the frontrunners in the Democratic primary. Once again, I was a strong supporter of Dennis Kucinich. His platform spoke to all of my core values and ideals; single-payer health care, immediate withdrawal from Iraq, abolishing the death penalty, ending the war or drugs, legalizing same-sex marriage, withdrawal from the WTO and NAFTA, gun control, clean energy, and the list goes on. Talk about voting my conscience!

The Democratic nomination ultimately went to the young, charismatic Senator from Chicago, Barack Obama. I liked him, not nearly as much as I liked Kucinich, but a lot more than I liked John Kerry four years ago. He was a brilliant public speaker with the ability to inspire and electrify a crowd. Anyone who came off articulate and intelligent would be a welcome change from our last president. He didn't seem quite as moderate and centrist as Hillary Clinton, but Obama was definitely a middle-of-the-road Democrat. Obama's running mate, Joe Biden, thrilled me less as a candidate in the primaries than Obama and Clinton did. Eight years ago I might not have cared much at all. After all, how important is the Vice Presidential candidate anyway? Unfortunately Vice President Dick Cheney had expanded the reach and powers of the office extensively over the last eight years; the VP candidate had become a much bigger deal. This would be highlighted by the announcement of the Republican Presidential nominee John McCain's choice for his running mate, the previously unknown Alaskan Governor, Sarah Palin.

At this point you may be saying to yourself "I thought this was going to be an essay about music, not about elections." Don't worry; I'm getting to the music part right about now! Around this time I had began working on the debut album for my new musical project, Golden Bloom. I had about three songs that were fully mixed and because if it's political themes, my publicist and I decided to release "The Fight at the End of the Tunnel" as the first digital single. Largehearted Boy, a music and literature website based out of Birmingham, AL had started to run a series of essays called "Why Obama". To quote Largehearted Boy writer and editor David Gutowski:

"Why Obama" is a series of guest essays by musicians and authors, where they share their support for Democratic United States presidential nominee Senator Barack Obama and offer arguments why he needs to be elected president of the United States.

Some previous contributors were Merge Records co-founder and Superchunk front man Mac McCaughan, Mighty Mighty Bosstones singer Dicky Barrett, Rilo Kiley bassist Pierre de Reeder, and Deerhoof drummer Greg Saunier. When my publicist told me that I had been asked to contribute an essay to the series I was very excited to be a part of this project. I felt strongly that electing Barack Obama as the 44th President of the United States would be the best outcome of this election, but the process of writing a "Why Obama" essay ended up being harder than I thought. I struggled with the outcome of not voting my conscience in 2004, and I felt obligated to highlight the areas where Barack Obama and I differed in opinion. Admittedly, it took about ten revisions before my "Why Obama" essay actually sounded like it was *supporting* Obama. In the end I'm quite proud of the finished product, which just happened to be published on Largehearted Boy's website on September 11th, 2008. I'd like to share that essay with you now:

We, the American people, are less than two months away from choosing our next president and at this time I find myself in a troubled spot. While my inner idealist would like to be writing a "Why Kucinich" essay right now, my inner pragmatist knows better. Anyone pushing for immediate withdrawal from Iraq and the impeachment of the war criminals that currently occupy the White House is not going to be the Democratic Presidential Nominee. It seems that every time an election rolls around it's "the most important election of our lives", but that may just be the truth this time.

For me, there are two major reasons why I will vote for Barack Obama in November. The first reason is that aside from a third term of Bush/Cheney, electing John McCain would be the worst thing that could happen to our nation and our so-called democracy. The second reason is the difference between FEAR and HOPE. We've spent the last eight years under the rule of fear. The Bush administration has kept us complacent by keeping us afraid, and with good reason. How else could we allow our own government to systematically disassemble the Bill Of Rights and strip us of our civil liberties unless we are crippled by fear? Barack Obama has and continues to instill hope in the hearts of the

133

disillusioned and disenfranchised. In such an imperfect world, where the changes that need to take place to restore our democracy and our good name in the world are HUGE, hope is what we need the most, because hope is the only thing that can set the wheels of change in motion.

There have been some bumps in the road where Obama and I have not seen eye to eye. There was the Protect America Act provision of the Foreign Intelligence Surveillance Act, or FISA, which allowed the Bush administration to spy on Americans without a warrant and granted retroactive immunity to the telecommunications companies doing the wire-tapping. Although Obama voted for the revised FISA bill that would end the Bush administration's illegal wire-tapping, the bill still granted immunity to the telecommunications companies. The very idea of telecom giants like AT&T and Verizon getting off with a warning for violating the Constitution has my inner idealist packing for Canada! Obama also supported the Supreme Court's decision to overturn the 32 year-old hand gun ban in Washington D.C. This was not the view on gun control that as a progressive I would have liked to hear.

One of the biggest issues for me personally is that of media consolidation. We live in a time where Monopoly is just a board game, where "The Big Six" (G.E., Time Warner, Disney, Viacom, CBS, and Rupert Murdoch's News Corp.) own virtually all of the TV, radio, print media, and online outlets that we get our news from. What this means is that we see, hear and read the news that the largest corporations in the world want us to see, hear and read. This, in essence, stifles our democracy because it limits what we know. I believe that people are well intentioned by nature and that the average American forms their opinions and bases their decisions on lack of information. If people were better informed I truly believe that our country would be a very different place. Barack Obama hasn't really made any public statement about his stance on media consolidation, and can you blame him? Howard Dean was a promising candidate until he made his views on media consolidation known. The result was his "Yee-haw Heard 'Round The World" which every major media outlet was more than happy to cram down our throats every minute or two. While John McCain hasn't verbally made his stance known, all you need to do is take a look at his staff. McCain's presidential campaign manager, his deputy campaign manager, his Senate chief of staff, campaign finance director, his national finance co-chairman, a campaign co-chairman, an unpaid chief adviser, and over a dozen McCain fundraisers have ALL been lobbyists for telecommunications companies. I think they send a pretty clear message about where McCain's priorities will be when it comes to media consolidation. If media consolidation isn't something you know much about and you want to learn more, I recommend checking out FreePress.net, reading Noam Chomsky's Media Control, and watching or listening to Democracy Now's daily news broadcast.

If there is anyone out there reading this who is truly inspired and energized by John McCain please chime in, but there is no denying that Barack Obama has done something that no other presidential candidate has done during the span of my political awareness. He has been able to make a person feel like they have the rare opportunity to vote for someone who is intelligent and caring, who really cares about them and their needs, and truly wants them to be part of the dialogue. Whether or not I agree with him every step of the way, I know that only someone who inspires hope can be the catalyst for real change. We have a long way to go to change the imperfect world we live in, one that is run by what John Perkins (author of Confessions of an Economic Hitman) calls the "corporatocracy", but we have to start somewhere. This may be the optimistic me silencing my idealistic side, but I believe that if we elect Barack Obama in November we have, at least, a fighting chance of making someone in the highest levels of government accountable to us, the hopeful, and hopefully informed Americans.

My band, Golden Bloom, has released a track called "The Fight at the End of the Tunnel" that will be on our upcoming album. The lyrics to the chorus of the song are "Remembering how *hard we fall, standing tall we're gonna get ready for the new day when there's one for all, standing tall we're gonna get ready for the new day." Although I didn't write this song about Barack Obama, in fact, I wrote the lyrics long before there were any presidential nominees, I feel like the message of the song is embodied by Obama's supporters, who truly are ready for a new day and are working incredibly hard to make that day come soon. I really do believe there is a fight at the end of the tunnel, because once Obama is elected, that's when the real work begins. That's when we all need to make our voices heard louder than ever, because there will finally be someone listening.*

This essay series wasn't the only place where musicians were voicing their support for Barack Obama's campaign. Artists were coming out of the woodwork left and right to help Obama's candidacy. Bands like Arcade Fire, Superchunk, The National, and Wilco all played campaign rallies and fundraisers, lending their music and their influence to the Democratic candidate. Bruce Springsteen even became Obama's "opening act" for several campaign events. When The Boss is warming up the stage for you, you know you're doing something right! Celebrities have always endorsed Presidential candidates, band and musicians being no exception. This time around it felt different though, there seemed to be more bands supporting Obama than there were for Gore and Kerry combined.

A month before the election I attended a "Barack Rock" benefit concert that friends of mine had organized at The Music Hall of Williamsburg in Brooklyn, NY. Andrew Bird, Franz Ferdinand, Les Savy Fav, Guster, and The Fiery Furnaces all lent their talents toward creating an amazing event. The collective hope and optimism in that room could have powered a small village, and we all felt like anything was not only possible, but within our reach. I don't need to tell you about the outcome of November 4th, 2008. I ran out of my apartment into the street, shouting exuberantly, and I wasn't alone. Cars drove by honking their horns in celebration. If a fireworks display were to have erupted in the sky it wouldn't have been the least bit out of place. *We* had done it, and I strongly emphasize *we*. No one factor could solely be attributed to Obama's victory; it was a culmination of a lot of hard work, and a lot of heart.

On January 19th, 2009, President Barack Obama was inaugurated in Washington D.C., and there was no shortage of music involved in the celebration. An estimated 400,000 people attended the "We Are One" concert at the Lincoln memorial the day before the inauguration, with performances by Beyonce, Mary J. Blige, Bono, Garth Brooks, Sheryl Crow, Josh Groban, Herbie Hancock, John Legend, Jennifer Nettles, John Mellencamp, Usher, Shakira, Bruce Springsteen, James Taylor, will.i.am and Stevie Wonder. Almost a dozen Inaugural balls took place on January 20th, 2009, with additional performances by The Dead and Jay-Z.

As I sit and write this essay, almost exactly two years later, I feel like I am standing alone at a concert. The band has left the stage, and the crowd is gone, yet I continue clapping my hands, waiting for an encore. As concertgoers, we have an expectation that after the band we paid to see leaves the stage, they will shortly return for an encore performance. I'm sure that some acts really make the audience "earn" that encore with applause, hoots and hollers, but for the most part it has come to be expected as part of the concert experience.

Democracy doesn't only happen during election cycles. Democracy requires participation, and that participation goes beyond electing our official representatives. The work doesn't stop after Election Day, in fact, that's when the real work starts. Our nation's youth were filled with hope and energy but the momentum seemed to die down quickly. We may have elected a candidate who campaigned on the message of hope and change, but we also elected a moderate Democrat, who received almost $1,000,000 in campaign donations from Goldman Sachs, almost $700,000 each from Citigroup and JPMorgan Chase, and over $500,000 from Morgan Stanley (according to the Center for Responsive Politics). Even though Obama also raised a record amount of donations from average American citizens, most of that energized base hung up their hat once Obama took office, and a dormant American public is no match for the lobbying power and influence of Wall Street and the financial industry. The Obama administration subsequently spent hundreds of billions of dollars bailing out the banks and financial institutions that caused problems themselves.

It wasn't just the bank bailout. There was continuous delay in closing the military prison at Guantanamo Bay, which was an Obama campaign promise. There was the refusal to allow any supporters of single-payer health care to take part in the debate on health care reform, resulting in a compromise of a bill that makes small improvements in our greatly flawed and immoral for-profit health care system. There was the refusal to investigate and prosecute members of the Bush administration who admitted to allowing the torture of prisoners at Abu Ghraib and Guantanamo. There was the extension of the Bush era tax cuts for all Americans, including the top 2%, and the extension of the estate tax exemption for up to $10,000,000. Where were all the voices for hope and change? I felt like I was alone at the concert after everyone had left, and there was no encore.

I strongly believe that the bands and musicians who rallied their support behind Barack Obama during the campaign had a profound effect on the outcome of the election. If even half of the musicians and artists who played a role in Obama's victory maintained their presence in our political discourse our nation would be in a different place right now. I don't want to insinuate that bands shouldn't help a candidate, and I am in no way criticizing any celebrities who helped support Obama. I do want to propose however that if more bands used their influence to inform their fans about issues and proposed legislation, encouraged their fans to write to and call their Senators and Congressional Representatives, they could play a big part in putting more power in the hands of the people, which is where it belongs. Musicians can make a huge impact on our democracy because democracy and music both depend so heavily on participation.

A perfect example of bands wielding their power of influence is Reverb, an environmental non-profit organization started in 2004 by Guster guitarist Adam Gardner and his wife, Lauren Sullivan. According to their website:

Reverb provides comprehensive, custom greening programs for music tours while conducting grassroots outreach and education with fans around the globe. In addition to their greening work with bands and artists, Reverb also works to move forward the sustainable practices of music industry leaders, including venues, record labels, and radio stations.

Over the last six years, Reverb has greened almost 100 tours. They also launched the Green Music Group, a large-scale, high profile environmental coalition of musicians, industry leaders and music fans using their collective power to bring about widespread environmental change within the music industry and around the globe.

Imagine if the same thing were to be done for meaningful health care reform. What if bands united to call for an end to the wars in Iraq and Afghanistan? The possibilities are endless. Americans have demonstrated how powerful the message of hope and change can be, but we can't just wish for it, and we can't just vote for it. We have to *be* that hope and change, and only then can we truly begin to make the world a better place.

Shawn Fogel *performs under the moniker Golden Bloom, where he constructs intelligent, contemporary indie power pop. The singer and multi-instrumentalist is so fully committed to his music that when he records an album, he plays nearly every instrument himself; tracking layers of his own vocal melodies for some of the purest and most encouraging indie pop out today. In January of 2009, SPIN magazine featured Golden Bloom as an "undiscovered band worth a listen", His 2010 project Neutral Uke Hotel (a re-interpretation of Neutral Milk Hotel's seminal album In the Aeroplane Over the Sea) finds Fogel transforming one of his favorite albums entirely on the ukulele.*

The Fake Psychology of Music Blogging: The Epic Battle of Good vs. Evil

By Andy Fenstermaker

Hello, my name is Andy, and as of June 6, 2011 I will have consistently managed, operated, and owned a regularly-updated music blog for five years. The statement gives off a rather "Addicted Anonymous" vibe; in a way, that's fitting. Blogging in this manner is an addiction and an affliction. You get the rewards, but you also get the borderline mental conditions. And the latter is almost never a good thing.

Why would one want to put themselves through the torment and stress of running a digital publication as such? We put ourselves at risk of stress-induced cardiac arrest, and of countless other medical conditions, of which you will soon read. The benefits, the risks – oddly enough, they often commingle. And for what? The cred of being able to call yourself a "Music Blogger?" Can't anyone do that? Yes and no.

It's been well over a decade since taking Psychology 101, but I'll do the best self-diagnosis as is possible.

Indie Cred = Narcissism

I run a moderately popular music blog and, at times, this fact can go to my head. Ego comes with the territory. Saying *Yeah, I know so-and-so*, or *My friend blah-blah-blah* makes you feel special, like you've got a bit added credibility. But in truth, it's just boastful feelings of faux self-worth. It's triviality, at best.

What we are, in truth, are gatekeepers. We control what goes up – what gets play and what doesn't. Sometimes it's the luck of the draw, and at other times it's dependent purely on timing. This too gives off hints of narcissism.

Free Records = Hoarding

All you have to be is a fellow record collector and watch (or read) Nick Hornby's *Hi-Fidelity* to understand this one. In my own mind, I am Rob Gordon. Music paraphernalia covers my walls, fourteen 12" by 12" framed records surround my living room, equally spaced at eye level so if you slowly rotate 360 degrees while standing in the center you'll get a clear picture of both my musical preferences as well as some damn fine art.

I have a spare bedroom entirely devoted to more than 2000 LPs, over 500 7" singles, and probably close to 5000 compact discs. There are 100 show posters I have yet to afford framing or locate wall space for. And those counts were from two years ago. Oh yeah, and a giant bin filled with buttons and stickers from bands, labels, and music events.

It's often hard to part with some of the records, which come in at an astonishing rate. Music bloggers fill up their homes with artifacts that hold special meaning to them. Could I name every album in that room? I could try, and maybe I'll drop 1,500 albums onto a list before I get bored and put on *Marquee Moon* or *Tigermilk* and play with my cat.

Then there's the digital side of the affliction. You get so many emails from bands and friends of bands and promotion companies and record labels that it leaves your head spinning and splitting with minor migraines.

You get a trickle-down of advertising revenue, if you are lucky enough to have advertising. And a too-big cut of that goes right back out the door in taxes. The rest (and then some) gets spent on regular record diving trips to the local metropolitan area.

The income adds to the hoards of memorabilia.

Consistent Writer = Exhibitionist

Bloggers are notorious for putting it all out there, making their lives and the lives of those they love available for everyone to see. In a way we expose ourselves to our reader, and that makes us exhibitionists. We like it this way. It takes a certain personality to give yourself to the world, all your personality quirks, the good and the bad. Exhibitionism – Freud had to come in somewhere, after all. And that's all I'm going to say on that topic.

Career Advancement = Grandiose Delusion

We music bloggers delude ourselves into believing we are making a difference. It's true!

We feel we are credible sources, have used the music blog to gain relevant and valuable experience, and feel that, even though in its current state it's always in some form of imminent failure, our blogging will bring us some future opportunity.

Sure, I can say that my most valuable day jobs have ultimately stemmed from a mix of past experience, my degrees of higher education, and the fact that I'm a regular blogger of music – and that would be, to an extent, true.

But then again, is it? Am I just conjuring all this in my little head, elevating my status as a music blogger to grotesque grandiose levels?

An autobiographical interview:

Am I a better writer now that I blog about music?

Yes. I think so. Then again, who's to tell? I put punctuation marks outside of song titles like this: *My current favorite song by a Seattle band is The Head And The Heart's "Couer D'Alene".* Even looking at it, it doesn't seem right. But near five years of consistent writing *must* mean that my skills have progressed, my vocabulary increased, my ability to construct well-thought-out critical (yet overwhelmingly positive) narrative improved… right?

Can I call myself a Social Media Expert because I actively engage my readers in a blog, on Facebook and via Twitter?

143

I plead the fifth. No, not really. I am of the belief that you can't really call yourself an expert because social media is so big – sure, I'm skilled in these three areas, and I could create viable strategies for business via the medium, but the area itself is so new that you'd have to be Mark Zuckerberg or the guy who came up with Twitter or the head of Foursquare to truly call yourself an expert. After all, they're the ones bringing in millions, and FensePost is nowhere near to being a day job for me.

Enough. Autobiographical interview? That leads me to the next affliction.

Critic = Compulsive Liar

I call them album reviews, but what they really are is overly positive promotional soliloquies. I am a critic, I am a fanboy. Critic sounds so much more appealing, though. It has that edge to it, kind of like political commentator versus pundit. There's just something negative sounding about the latter of each of those labels.

Unfortunately, as much as I hate to say it, a lot of really, really great bands don't get included because there's simply not enough time nor editorial space to cover them all. Criticism, then, comes through via the gatekeeper. Is a band worthy of the blog. This question comes up a lot in music blogging. So why cover a band I do not like?

Liar comes in many forms. We say one thing one moment and looking back a month later, we wonder why we came to the conclusion we did. We contradict ourselves constantly. This was obvious in my retrospective best-of lists from 2009, in which I took the previous year's top albums and reorganized them based on additional years of existence. That's totally ridiculous, and I know it.

Blogger = Obsessive Compulsive

I have to blog. It's a nervous tick, like Charlie Kelly's mother tapping things three times so he won't die. Like the younger Kelly, I'd be apt to start doing it too, thinking *We'll, it's worked so far, might as well give it a try*. I cannot stop blogging. In fact, when I cut posts down from two per weekday to one per weekday in order to allow myself more time to work on restoring my '68 BMW 1600, I started blogging about *that* process. It has become an inherent part of my very being.

Reflection

So, what do you get for being a music blogger? You get an overly pretentious sense of delusional narcissism, complemented with OCD and hoarding.

This is something I have come to recognize and accept in myself. As they say, the first step to tackling your addiction is to recognize it as such. While I'm not ready to overcome the blogging nor the afflictions that come with it, I accept their presence.

It is who I am, and I like who I am. And deep down, yes… I hope you do to.

Andy Fenstermaker is the founder of Fensepost.com, a blog based in the fertile tulip and potato-filled lands between Seattle, WA and Vancouver, BC. He lives and breathes for music. He spends his days in a more lucrative career field, but he always comes home to a loving girlfriend and well organized collection of vinyl. He also likes to restore older model BMW's in the garage of his Mt. Vernon home.

You Don't Need Money, You Don't Need Fame
By Scott Taylor

I play guitar because of Huey Lewis & The News.

Well…I play guitar because of Huey Lewis, The News AND a diminutive Michael J. Fox sporting a vest & jean jacket combo, desiring a 4x4 and an ever-understanding girlfriend, and shredding unholy hotlicks for baffled and beguiled 1950s teenagers while on his knees. Which is to say, I play guitar because of a movie. But that isn't quite right.

So perhaps I play guitar because of the "power of love." But, my god, man, that sounds wildly unforgivable.

And perhaps it's in my best interest to provide the necessary background and rationale before making any further hasty declarations. Here goes:

Each awkward adolescent morning, on a bus delivering me to a small Catholic elementary school in South Jersey, I would impulsively play, flip and repeat the cassette tapes containing the mid-to-late 1980s output of one Huey Lewis and his News. Specifically, the albums *Sports, Fore!* and *Small World* were spun ragged on a series of Walkmans that were constantly breaking down and devouring AA batteries at an ungodly rate. (I'll try my best to keep God out of this from here on out. It won't work. I went to Catholic school. I've stated this twice now.) It was on those Walkmans, placed deliberately to my right and hidden by my jacket and book bag combo, where I would devotedly strum every guitar chord and flat pick every solo contained within those three albums. They were gospel to me. The Bible, most assuredly, was not. (Sorry, God.)

I breathed and deeply felt every bluesy harmonica riff, every rubbery romantic sentiment, every austere life affirmation, every blustery saxophone solo, every artful keyboard flourish, every understated bass groove and every manic, freaked-out solo. Especially those solos. The News guitarist, Chris Hayes, did spectacular things to my body in those days – sending chills cruising through my 7 (and 8 and 9 and 10) year-old frame at such alarming speeds and sensations that I was bound to wonder, but petrified to ask, if anyone else experienced such similar vibrations (perhaps while reading The Bible?). It was during "Power of Love" that I first felt moved by a flurry of guitar notes. It was while watching Michael J. Fox duck walk across a cinema screen while miming "Johnny B. Goode" when I realized what I wanted to do with the rest of my life.

The best way to fulfill this destiny, I decided, was to enter the school talent show in 3rd grade and put on display for the entire student body the full memorizing arsenal of my guitar hubris. My only obstacle was that I had no idea how to play guitar. But thanks to my constant bus-riding mimicry, I sure as shit knew how to air guitar – of which lip synching was a very close cousin.

I managed to coax a giant red hollow body from a girl whom I had a crush on (she was entirely too tall for me to be voicing such feelings). It was her dad's, closet-tucked and dusty, when I convinced my mom to take me to her house to retrieve it under the guise of a group project we were supposed to be working on. I spent the rest of that afternoon opening up the case and staring down at it, amazed that something as exotic as a guitar was now in my possession – if only temporarily. "Do you know how to play it?" Theresa asked expectantly. "A little," I said and tried to act as cool as an 8-year old holding an outrageously oversized, out-of-tune guitar can.

When the day of the talent show appeared, nerves were rocket high. I had spent the previous three nights sleepless and dancing in front of a mirror while lip synching to a non-stop loop of "Power of Love." I knew the words, I knew the changes, I knew my big solo. But how would I perform under pressure? There would be a lot of quick judging eyes upon me (thankfully, my brother had graduated to high school the previous year) and very little maneuvering room for mistakes. I would be all alone up there with only a microphone standing between me and 106 (I counted) peers.

I was most nervous about wetting my pants. Or forgetting how to move. Or wetting my pants and forgetting how to move. Luckily, I had a giant guitar to cover-up any potential spillage.

When it was my time to go on, I climbed the stage uneasily and tried to unfocus my eyes on all the others staring back at me. I nodded to the nun in charge and she hit play on the tape that I had put an incredibly inordinate amount of time in making certain was properly synched up. The first couple of seconds were stiff, to be sure, and the butterflies in my stomach threatened to make themselves visible all over the stage floor. But then I caught a groove. I thought back to the bus. I thought back to my room. I thought back to the future. And I started to move.

I welded that guitar like a hot animal ready to strike out at any moment. I pumped the neck up and down to cue section changes. I ran my fingers around the fret board at such a frenzied pace that I amazed even myself. I made faces. I struck poses. I was reborn in the form of a guitar god befit of worship, even if I was producing no actual sound. And when that solo came, I got on my knees, and then my back, and squirmed across that stage like a repentant serpent.

By the time the music stopped, I was sweatier than any kid ever should be and my heart was an overworked locomotive. When I looked up, kids clapped. Loudly. Some of them even hooted and hollered. I was a hit. I was….rock 'n' roll.

My only other challenger for the 3rd grade trophy was a kid who planned to put on a karate exhibition. Apparently, there was a movie that popularized this activity at the time. Sure, karate was cool. But was it really cooler than Huey Lewis and The News? Or me?

The answer is, yes. Yes, it is.

I came in second. Out of two.

When I think back, it pains me to picture a tiny, unruly haired, mousey voiced version of me pretending his Walkman is a cream colored Strat while cranking Dad rock at peak levels with the aid of orange Styrofoam headphones. Or prancing across a giant colorless stage aping Michael J. Fox aping Chuck Berry. But I do wish I had video of such occurrences. If only for my own private viewing.

It's taken me 32 years and I still can't play a solo as perfectly paced and peaked-out as those 30 seconds that Chris Hayes unloads upon "Power of Love." But I'll keep trying until I do. And, until then, I'll always have a bedroom mirror and Huey Lewis and The News.

Scott Taylor *sang and played guitar in the recently retired No Go Know, along with a myriad of other unheard-of bands. He lives hipsterly in Portland, OR with his wife and step-daughter, and is currently recording the dreaded SOLO ALBUM in between bouts of a flooded basement and fantasy basketball.*

You Are the Words, I Am the Tune, Play Me
By Michael W. Nestor, Ph.D.

"John said, 'My arms get really tired sometimes, and my heart pounds. It is like my body is made of rubber with this beating, pounding heart reverberating against the bands. When I get to the top of the flight of stairs with my heavy amp, I can't remember if my heart pounds from the work, or from the excitement I feel knowing that I get to connect with them again, to feel their energy. Either way, I remember the van, and the miles, and the conversation, and most of all-the anticipation'." *–Journal entry from The Seldon Plan's tour journal, 1/14/10*

Many people will try to tell you how to make your music work, and how to try to make money in this modern amalgam of social networking and free downloads. Some will tell you that the music industry is dead. "No one pays for music anymore". Some will argue that music now is more alive than ever with buzzwords like "freemium model", "organic search marketing", or "democratization of music distribution". Finally, there are those who think that the song will always speak for itself, and the cream will always rise to the top and be recognized no matter what economic model exists.

I believe that musicians and those who help to distribute music should always be progressive, forward thinking, and optimistic. However, I don't think that a life in independent music is about any of the ideas that I just reviewed. Independent music is really about local ecosystems, about making tangible connections with your neighbors, and cultivating long term relationships that don't always center on music. A life in indie music is really story creation - it is the un-written autobiography of your journey through lives that interconnect, and the adventures that connect them make all the time and sacrifice worthwhile.

The act of creating art is both a public and private venture. Private in the sense that that art reflects some deep connection to the hidden psyche of the artist-yet the public airing of that creation is what gives it lasting meaning by connecting it with a larger zeitgeist. In lieu of adding more text to the "how to make it in indie music" conversation, I thought the reader might get something out of the personal story behind my creation of my own independent record label. Hopefully these personal stories will inspire and motivate those readers who feel that they must create and distribute music in order to exist-but also must reconcile the economic realities of such an existence.

The Beechfields Record Label Story

The inspiration for the label was really a moment in time. There was a special moment in music from about 1993-1998 when hip hop, rock, pop were allowed to flow free from the underground scene to the radio and people's ears. This was because the system was flush with label money and the big labels were really into artist development at the grassroots level. This was the time when it was not uncommon to see shows where bands like The Poster Children, Acetone, Archers of Loaf, and Hum, Velocity Girl, Tuscadero, Hazel etc were right next to large label-heavy acts like Nirvana, or Stone Temple Pilots, or even Soundgarden.

There was tangibility about that time - where a band could make a great record, play a bunch of shows and have a reasonable chance of getting seen/heard. I mean, my own band at the time Man of the Atom opened for Karate, a band that I had a ton of admiration for and we were nobodies. I remember seeing Jawbox open for Stone Temple Pilots at George Mason University and the crowd was dumbfounded-but that sort of cross-pollination and discovery was possible during that era because people were willing to explore and the industry was open to spending money. In addition, there was not a ridiculous saturation of bands, like you have now with the advent of home recording and the internet.

At the time, I was a huge admirer of Simple Machines and met Jenny Toomey once and she was great. I started making my own hand-made cassettes when I was in high school, copied off of their hand-made stuff with my own twist. I used to record everything in my basement with a $20 Radio Shack omni-directional microphone and a used beat up 4-track Tascam cassette tape recorder. I would write songs and try to emulate bands like The Spinannes (who were my biggest inspiration for my own music and the label-I just loved the home-made feel of their records and songs), Peach, Sunny day Real Estate, Placebo, and The Smashing Pumpkins.

Because I lived in a small town (at the time) there were only 4 or 5 other kids who knew about these bands-and so when I started making my tapes as "Pupa's Window", they were traded pretty quickly around my high school and to my surprise really liked (mainly because these kids didn't know the influences-so this was new to them, and this was before "emo" and "indie" and all that). I learned all the recording techniques to stretch 4 tracks into 8 and so on. I also listened to a ton of jazz and new age music (I used to ferociously listen to a show called "Hearts of Space" on our local NPR station) and I started putting spacey, ambient stuff and samples between the songs...it was a big hit. This really shaped my approach to records.

The local bands I had in mind when I started the label were Ida (they moved to NY), Grenadine, The Exploder, Third Harmonic Distortion, and Rainer Maria. Actually, the idea for the label was formed in my mind in 1999 when I saw The Exploder open for Rainer Maria at the UMBC "She Plays Bass" cafe in the basement of the Patapsco dorm that happened every Thursday night. It was the best show I have ever seen (I mean right in front of The Exploder would take your breath away)...and I thought,"I want to do that." I quickly realized that Baltimore did not have a place for this sort of music and the world of music was retracting into Napster-so I knew that I was at the wrong place and the wrong time to look to others to do it-so I started The Beechfields.

From the beginning of the label, I have been about making physical records that come with artwork and have emphasized that they should be as special as possible. That is because I grew up listening to vinyl and also during the indie mixtape/hand-made cassette era-so art is important to me, and so are hand-made records. To this day-we try to stay true to that ethic. As the label has come up against the iTunes takeover of music, we have had to fight the rising tide of people just wanting a digital download in lieu of a real CD. Setting aside all the issues with how crappy MP3s sound as compared to a real CD, it became clear that over the past couple of years, digital was winning. Thus, I had to come up with an acceptable way to release things digitally, but still maintain some connection with my roots.

I had been reading about microfinance because I have been trying to design a way to increase science education in poor communities using it. I was really disappointed with the state of American science progress and funding when I finished my doctorate. So I became a consultant with The Human Brain Project in order to design a system that used microfinance in that context-to allow local communities to fund science research, thus creating a bridge between citizens and the labs in their community.

When The Beechfields faced our digital dilemma, I decided that I wanted to allow people to use the microfinance model when it came to the label-in order to allow more connections between my label and the community we work in. In return for their monetary support on current records, I have offered listeners free digital versions of our back catalog with downloadable art and liner notes. I also opened up this exchange to our artists so that they can release "digital only" releases but still make them special.

Hopefully, you appreciate that crafting your own story using what you know and with the support of people who care for you and your dreams is the only way "to make it" in indie music. If you see something that needs to be done, do it. If you want to make the music industry a better place for yourself and others, then make your local scene better. Create and cultivate out of self interest balanced heavily with a viewpoint for advancing the cause of others.

Yes, the democratization of music means that there are millions more boats on an already crowded sea. It also gives more power to those who have the biggest boats and the loudest megaphones. But the old cliché still holds true-that a rising tide lifts all boats. Independent music requires *you* to be that rising tide. A strong direction sense that is guided by the artistic dreamer in you, coupled by the pragmatism you also have in your head, will make you a beacon for others. It is in this service to others, through sharing your music but most importantly, through helping others share theirs, that you will find true independence and happiness navigating the new landscape that has been crafted by our generation for the future of music.

Michael W. Nestor, Ph.D. *is a neuroscientist, musician, and mastering engineer from Baltimore, MD. In 2003 he founded The Beechfields Record Label, a not-for-profit artist-centered label that focuses on high-quality indie-pop records and a supportive community-centered approach to music. As a musician, he has toured nationally and released records on the Magnatune Label as part of The Seldon Plan and solo as Pupa's Window. His focus in the world of indie music is on using non-traditional economic models (e.g. micro-finance and freemium approaches) to support and distribute local music to local markets. When not in the studio or working on the label, Michael is in the laboratory applying cellular neuroscience techniques to search for molecular mechanisms underlying Autism and Schizophrenia. He has published book chapters and scholarly articles on the role of changes in astrocytic morphology and dendritic spine morphology on synaptic physiology. He currently works on the role of dendritic excitation on learning and memory in the mammalian brain.*

Racing Stripes
By Michael Phillips

In the autumn of 2007 my former band broke up and I emerged from the disastrous cloud that had engulfed my mid-twenties to discover I was poor, exhausted, bloated, hung over and momentarily shell shocked from a fresh new introduction to reality.

I had spent the previous two years trying to make it in a rock band, following a dream I'd had for years and we put every ounce of our soul into the project. It was as you might imagine, some of the best times of my life.

Yet three years after our sudden implosion I find myself doing something completely different. I'm working a 9-5 office job, playing folk music and I am ok with that.

As distinguished people have noted millions of time throughout history, failing is part of a process that moves you towards your greater calling and it's often hard to know what that greater calling is. It also helps to keep your greater calling flexible and to make exceptions when necessary.

Sometimes people force their greater calling and it's just as foolish as a five year old proclaiming he wants to be a police officer while still young enough to feel uninhibited donning underwear stained with racing stripes.

I have to believe that the reason I never "made it" is because that band wasn't part of my plan. Certainly that statement is tinged with a little new age woo-woo magic, but underneath that statement is the belief that when you are doing things that conflict with your personal values, you are destined to fail. It sounds obvious, but if you don't know what I am talking about then just you wait.

In hindsight everything is obvious.

I was forgoing many important personal friendships, standards and values to prioritize success as a musician - and if I had only pulled my head out of my ass for a minute, I probably would have realized that my "little engine that could" attitude was carelessly plodding along face-first into a brick wall.

155

Our brief two-year career begun in January 2006 and by the end of 2007 the reverie had become like the ill-fated Deep Horizon gulf oil rig and I was among three castaways at sea - baffled and desperately clinging to splintered dreams.

All too often we agreed to disagree in order to resolve deep seeded conflicts, problems which only seemed to be compounded after spending two summer months living together in a van. We were certainly different people and we all had things to learn about ourselves. We made bad decisions, we had ideological differences, we didn't trust one another. Within two months of returning from our first national tour, two of us were presented with an inflexible and unfavorable band agreement from the singer/songwriter. He presented it as trying to protect his interests but it wasn't fair and immediately brought all the underlying tensions to surface and before we knew it, the band was no more.

It happened just like that.

Some people feel like you only get one shot to make it in this world, but that's bullshit. There are many paths towards happiness and definitions of success and you just need to find out what works for you. If I could offer any bit of advice based on my experience it's that you need to choose your friends wisely and have confidence in what you do. Sure, the chances are good that you'll fail or become sidetracked, but you'll be on the right path so long as you're always following your heart.

Michael Phillips *works for a branding/marketing firm in Portland, Oregon where he has lived for the past six years. He currently moonlights with four of his best friends on a side project to life called The Fenbi International Superstars, which was nominated for a 2009 Portland Music Award.*